A Practical Guide to:

Publishing Books Using Your PC

To Sarah, Aleksander, Charlotte and Daniel

A Practical Guide to:

Publishing Books Using Your PC

Organising, Writing, Printing and Marketing Your Own Books

Peter Domanski and Philip Irvine

First Edition

Domanski-Irvine Books

British Library Cataloguing-in-publication data

A catalogue record for this book is available from the British Library.

Copyright © 1997 by Peter Domanski and Philip Irvine

Published by Domanski-Irvine Book Company, Coldwell Farm, Stretfordbury, Leominster, Herefordshire HR6 0QL, United Kingdom.
email info@dibookco.u-net.com

ISBN 0-952-60432-9

First Edition 1997

Note. Although the authors have researched the material presented in this book as thoroughly as possible, we assume no responsibility for errors, omissions or inaccuracies contained therein. No liability can be accepted for any losses or expenses incurred as a result of relying on information given. We strongly advise seeking professional legal advice if in any doubt about laws related to publishing. Legal obligations and restrictions outside the UK may well differ markedly from those that apply in the UK.

Typeset, printed and bound by Domanski-Irvine Books.

PREFACE

📖 Have you skills, ideas or specialised knowledge you wish to communicate to others?
📖 Have you a story or some poetry to tell?
📖 Have you considered publishing your work?

Despite promises of a 'paperless' society and much vaunting of 'electronic' books, there has been a huge growth in paper-based books, magazines, journals, newsletters, etc. and there appears to be little end in sight of this current boom. There are publications, both general and specialised, that cover just about every niche in contemporary society and, far from saturation, there is a vast public appetite for news, articles, stories and information. We therefore suggest that from being just a *consumer*, you, the reader might like to develop your creative talents and consider becoming a *producer* - infinitely more rewarding!

So how will you proceed? You could approach an established publisher who, providing they find sufficient commercial merit in your project, may be interested in your ideas. However, even if your work is considered of a high standard and worthy of publication, you will be in competition with a host of other would-be authors so your chances of succeeding are very small unless you have a proven track record or are extremely lucky. Of course, there are a number of success stories about famous authors who were finally accepted after many rejections, but these are few and far between. As an alternative, you may consider joining an ever increasing number of people who have become publishers in their own right - and, if extra income is part of your motive, you will be able to retain substantially more of the cover price of your book than if you were using an established publisher - this is providing you can successfully produce and market your work effectively.

The idea for this book came about after successfully publishing our first book on the subject of computerised database design which has now sold in over 20 countries despite a virtually zero advertising budget. We would have saved much time and expense if we knew then what we know now. We very much hope that others might benefit from our experiences which are distilled into this book. We describe proven methods by which you can produce your own books and by taking the reader step by step through the major processes from writing to marketing. We believe we have covered in appropriate detail, all the significant concepts and factors required for successful publication. We hope to have struck a balance between being, on the one hand, too prescriptive and on the other, advising in vague generalities, a trap which is all too easy to fall into. Also, wherever possible, we have tried to de-mystify processes and avoid unnecessary jargon which abound in the worlds of computers and publishing.

The rapid evolution in software packages such as DTP (Desk Top Publishing) and the power and affordability of Personal Computers (PCs) and their peripherals now provides a practical and inexpensive route to independent publishing. Moreover, modern communications and distribution methods have largely overcome the self-publisher's perennial problem of reaching their market without experience of the publishing industry and a deep pocket for publicity. If you already own, or have access to a PC, there are now a range of publishing options available to you. Hand in hand with the ever growing sophistication and 'user friendliness' of computer technology, has been a dramatic fall in real costs so, at the present time, £1000 or less worth of equipment will provide you with all that you need to be able to start publishing from home, school, office or wherever.

Effective marketing of a book is vital and so, alongside conventional methods, we describe the means for creating your 'presence' on the Internet - a vast network of individuals and organisations - again at very low cost. The growing popularity of the Internet and World Wide Web as a means of communication, for promoting and conducting trade, enables you to create a 'shop front' accessible to over 40 million (1997 estimate) people world-wide. For publishers, whether large or small, organisations or individuals, the Internet represents both a new and rapidly growing market which is now rivalling traditional marketing methods.

The conventional printing process uses ink on paper. This basic principle has not changed for several hundred years but the means by which the printing plates are created have changed radically since the advent of computerisation. This process is available to the self-publisher and is recommended for relatively large print runs. However, there are now alternative means of producing the printed page. The development of laser printers and photocopiers has been rapid and their quality improved to the extent that they can also be used for book production. Whilst unit production costs may still be higher than the traditional printing method, the cost of purchase of a laser printer or hire of a photocopier is now so affordable that they can be an ideal route for the author / publisher to start producing books - particularly for a specialist market.

We believe that problems of preparation, production, communication and distribution are now very much diminished so the critical factors for success are now your own imagination and determination to succeed. If you can produce a product which is of merit, will be enjoyable to read or of interest and value to others then there is no insuperable barrier to succeeding and, as John Ruskin said, *"If a book is worth reading, it is worth buying "*.

Through our own personal experience, we have found that self-publishing is immensely satisfying giving authors / publishers a great sense of achievement. ….And, when those sales orders start to come in for your first book ….you can start thinking about writing the next one!

Table of Contents

Conventions

Prices: Please Note

The authors have endeavoured to present realistic equipment prices current at the time of publication (1st July 1997) which, unless stated otherwise, are exclusive of UK VAT (currently 17.5%). However, computer hardware costs are volatile and there is a 'rule' that states: "Prices halve and power doubles every 12 months." Whilst this may not be quite true, please bear in mind the rapid changes in both price and performance of PCs and other peripherals. As a consequence price information may quickly become out of date.

Finger Points

 Finger points contain important or useful facts or hints that should be noted.

Tip Boxes

Tip: A tip box contains information which is a time-saving or helpful short-cut. It gives advice that the reader may find useful.

1. Introduction

This book describes how you, the reader, can enter the world of publishing for minimal financial outlay. This can be achieved by taking advantage of the recent developments in computing technology which are now readily available. Ideally, having bought or borrowed this book, you will already have the beginnings of an idea for writing and/or publishing your own work; you may even have a manuscript prepared. Alternatively, you may be exploring ideas for using your PC for profit. There is money to be made from publishing but, a warning, do not believe that just because the mechanics of publishing have become easier, the process as a whole will be straightforward. It would be unwise to embark on a publishing venture *solely* with the intention of making money, for, besides the actual mechanics of preparation and printing, much thought and hard work is required to make a success out of even the most modest of projects.

1.1 Why Become Your Own Publisher?

Possible reasons *for* using an established publisher

- They have all the relevant technology at their disposal and will produce a first class product.
- You need only produce a manuscript; preparation for printing and most of the artwork will be done by the publisher.
- Your manuscript will receive careful editorial treatment and peer review for accuracy, style and quality of content.
- Marketing, distribution and sales will all be undertaken by the publisher and their agents. They obviously have a strong vested interest in your work's financial success.

Some reasons for *not* using an established publisher

- Your work may not be of sufficient commercial interest to a publisher - particularly if the subject is very specialised; they are not attracted by small or very small print runs.
- It may have been rejected by one or more publishers but you are determined to see it in print.

- If you are paying to see your work in print (vanity press), it can be prohibitively expensive.
- Although you may derive much personal satisfaction from seeing your work in print, you are unlikely to profit financially directly by this means as the proportion of the cover price which constitutes the author's royalties is normally only a small percentage (6-10%) of the *net* sales revenues.

Some Reasons *for* Self-Publishing

- You have complete control; editorial, production, distribution, marketing, etc.
- The equipment (hardware and software) you need has never been so sophisticated and so affordable; you may well already possess it and extra investment, if required, will be minimal.
- It can provide high levels of personal satisfaction and can bring you into contact with many interesting people - from service providers to customers.
- It can be very profitable - even for relatively low volume sales because you have ownership and control throughout the whole procedure with no 'middlemen'.
- You have a variety of production methods available to you and can 'cut your cloth according to your means'.
- You may be able to profit handsomely from low volume but high value publications typical of very specialised subjects, e.g., professional reports, instruction guides, data sources, etc.
- You may see publishing as a new business venture, maybe using skills and equipment that you already have.
- Publishing a book in your own specialised field may enhance your employability (e.g., as a consultant) as it demonstrates your expertise and credibility.
- In a specialist field, you may well understand your niche market (academe, professional body, etc.) better than a conventional publisher and be more likely to succeed in effective marketing.
- On an altruistic note, you can perhaps offer a service to others within your local community.

1.2 Motivation

It is worthwhile considering what motivates someone to want to write *and* publish a book. Taking on the role of both author *and* publisher requires much determination and dedication. Much effort will be expended planning, researching, writing, communicating, negotiating and learning a variety of new skills so the commitment of time and effort should not be underestimated. Even after the publication and launch of your book, your labours are not complete, for as a publisher you will need to become advertiser, distributor and bookkeeper. This makes for a long-term commitment. We will not make a drudge out of this as it can be tremendously rewarding but, be aware of the labours ahead! Below we list some motives:

- Redundancy: you have skills, experience, knowledge and time to spare, now you can use them for yourself rather than for your employer!
- Retirement: similarly, you have a career's worth of experience. Can you capitalise on this?
- Desire or need to create extra income - necessity is the mother of invention! Spurred on by the overdraft, taxman or mortgage?
- Community spirit: you may be able to organise a joint enterprise for a local charity or organisation.
- An enthusiastic interest in a specialist subject for which you may be an authority.
- Making a mark on posterity: your works will out-live you.
- It is said that, "Everyone has a book in them", you would like to get yours out of you!
- Self-advancement: it may help your career as a book will demonstrate your expertise; it may enable you to obtain work as consultant or lecturer; it will certainly enhance your c.v.
- Competitive spirit: "So and so has done it, I can do better", you have greater knowledge or a better story.
- Realising self-fulfilment: the completion of a major task and the satisfaction of success: a boost for ego and confidence.
- The expression of a creative talent: a book is tangible evidence of your creativity.
- You have been commissioned: someone is paying you to do it as they need your knowledge and experience.
- New business venture: yes, you can create a successful business out of specialist publishing - especially if you are capitalising on existing skills and resources.

- 📖 Capitalising on existing resources: "How can I make a return on the investment in my PC equipment and skills? "
- 📖 A "calling": an inspiration.
- 📖 Shortened life expectancy: can I leave a legacy to my children, grandchildren and friends? My life story, reminiscences, etc.
- 📖 Kudos: you seek the attention and acclamation of your peers!
- 📖 A desire to communicate, making knowledge available to a wide audience.

An understanding of your motives for publishing is very important for quite practical reasons. If, for example, the primary reason for embarking on such a project is to start a new business venture, the way in which you choose your subject, style your book and its contents will be 'market-lead'. You should, therefore, try to align your product to the demand of your market niche *(see chapter 8)*. If, on the other hand, you are co-ordinating a project for your local community, say the history of your village, you may be less inclined to try and please a national or international market.

1.3 Subjects

The saying, "There is a book in everybody" may be true but in the vast majority of cases we will never know what that book is. If you have already made up your mind about the subject and content of your book then fine, go for it! However, as author, publisher, marketeer and bookseller you will find that there are conflicting interests. As author, you may want your artistic freedom but as bookseller you may find that your subject has very little interest to others and so sales could be minimal. *If you are looking to publishing as a new business venture, you must have your eye on the market and adjust your subject matter to stand a good chance of selling books to get a return on your investment in time, money and effort.*

1.3.1 Works of fiction

For the small publisher, success for works of fiction is more difficult to achieve than for non-fiction. This is not necessarily due to inferior writing, or poor quality production but the great difficulty in breaking into a literary market already crowded by a continuous supply of new books (approximately 55,000 new titles a year). There is a reluctance by most readers to try out new authors unless highly praised by a handful of literary critics working for the national press, radio and television. When visiting a library, as a borrower, you are more likely to choose a novel by an author you have heard of. However, when selecting non-fiction, you look for an appropriate title and good coverage of the desired subject matter. Success in fiction is most likely if:

- 📖 You have already published and have a public following.

- 📖 You are able to bring your work to the attention of critics in literary circles, reviewers on national newspapers and other media - and are well received.
- 📖 You have a deep pocket for national advertising and creating 'hype'.
- 📖 You have an effective and responsive distribution network.
- 📖 You are a celebrity, famous or infamous.

Failing these criteria, you need not become despondent; there are some famous antecedents. In the UK, Virginia Woolf set up the Hogarth Press to publish her works and in the US Mark Twain published Huckleberry Finn privately. Other noted literary stars who self-published include Walt Whitman, Anaïs Nin, Gertrude Stein and James Joyce. In more recent times, there have been a number of success stories, particularly in the USA. Remember that your project can be financially rewarding even with a comparatively small number of sales. The challenge will be to find an outlet for your work and apply sufficient imagination and cunning to get noticed. For example, your work may belong to a niche genre such as Science Fiction, Horror, Crime, Romance, etc. Each of these specialities may have their own particular marketing outlet, e.g. specialised book clubs, magazines, societies, etc. By careful marketing strategy, you may be able to gain popularity in a niche market from which you can gain sales, confidence and cash. Further success can then be built on, by exploring other channels.

Poetry
Poetry has been undergoing a tremendous revival in recent years and now has an enthusiastic live performance circuit and there are now a number of thriving poetry magazines and societies. By publishing their work, new poets can hasten recognition and enhance their chances of being asked to read at live events. These occasions are ideal opportunities to promote their writings. As with lecturing and consultancy, this is a virtuous circle for the budding author and publisher - sales promote recognition that promotes sales!

1.3.2 Works of non-fiction
It is in this area that the author and self-publisher is most likely to find the greatest success. In effect, you are packaging and marketing information. If your information has broad appeal, then there is no reason why you should not be able to market it. Success will largely depend upon the nature and quality of your work but also upon:

- 📖 Your ability to attract attention to your 'product'(marketing).
- 📖 Your profit margin.
- 📖 Your ability to compete in the market.
- 📖 Your ability to match production to demand.
- 📖 Your means of distribution.

The following is a short list of subjects where small independent publishers have been successful - reflecting fashions in current consumer demand:

Animal husbandry	Local & regional subjects
Architecture	Natural History
Boats & sailing	'New Age' & alternative life style
Business guides	Pets
Children's books	Practical guides
Computing	Specialist travel itineraries (e.g. Food
Collectors subjects	& Drink)
Cooking and recipes	Professional guides
Curriculum textbooks	Religion
Educational books and tutors	Self-help, various therapies
Gardening	Sports
Hobbies and crafts	Survival guides
'How to' books	Science
Information sourcebooks	Technical manuals
Internet	

See under marketing for staying ahead of the competition

1.4 The Publishing Process

To take a project through all the stages to a successful outcome careful planning is required. The major steps are listed below:

Stage	Description	Decisions
The Muse	Ideas and inspiration	Will I publish and how?
	Market Research	Will I have a ready market, create one or am I unconcerned?
Planning	Planning the document.	What kind of PC equipment will I need?
		Which DeskTop package is best suited to my needs?
	Financial plan for the project; decide your budget	How much will the venture cost? What kind of returns can I expect?
	Determine timescales	How long will it take? What 'milestones' should I plan?
The Writing Process	Creating the skeleton or 'storyboard'	Can I give balance to the contents or fully summarise the plot?
	Composition	What material should I use?

	First review of material	Do I need any copyright permissions? Who will do my proof- reading? Who will give me an honest opinion?
Document Finalising	Format	What will be the format of my book A4, A5 other?
	Style	Headings/ Fonts/ type sizes/ Indents/ text alignment/ figures/ colour
	Components	Title Pages/ Forward/ Preface/ TOC/ Body of Document/ Index/ Appendices?
	Proof-reading, peer review and legal checks	Is it grammatically correct and does it transgress any laws?
Publishing Requisites	Registration as a publisher	What publishing title should I use and what address?
	Obtain ISBN	Title of Publication and summary for inclusion in book lists, etc.
Materials & Production	Choice of materials	Hardback or Paperback? Paper quality?
	Printing method	Is this dictated by a limited budget?
	Cover	Cover material? Design and production?
	Binding	Perfect/ Stitched/ Other?
	Packaging	Will I need any?
Marketing Strategy	Market research	Is my market purely local, national or international? Can I make use of the Internet? Retail or Direct Sales?
	Volume of stock	How many books will I need? Is this figure compatible with my means of production and budget?
	Financial matters	Have I organised my order processing and distribution? Financial record keeping? Bank Accounts?
	Advertising	What budget do I have? Will it be funded by initial sales?
Forward Planning	Maximising your return	How can I reduce costs? Do I need to increase my production?

1.5 The Technology

If you do not consider yourself technologically minded and have had little or no experience with computers - do not be daunted. You will be using a PC really as a high specification typewriter and mastering the basic skills is not difficult. Even if you have special needs because of disability such as poor sight or difficulty with a standard keyboard, there are specialised devices available to overcome such problems, e.g. voice activated text entry and editing control software is now available. (See *Ability* magazine in appendix.)

Several technological revolutions have occurred over the past few years that are dramatically affecting the way in which we work and communicate. The advances in computer technology both with 'hardware' and 'software', have been immense and are having an impact on many areas of our lives. The proliferation of Personal Computers within industry, commerce, education and the home is now so widespread that virtually all offices, schools and factories are equipped with PCs and ancillary equipment.

What are all these PCs being used for? Well, obviously, for a wide range of applications but there are the few that dominate:

- *Word Processing (WP) and Desktop Publishing (DTP)* for letter and document production.
- *Spreadsheets* - for data retention, analysis and presentation.
- *Databases* - for higher volumes of data storage and analysis.
- *Communication* - electronic mail (e-mail), information sharing through shared databases, ...and the Internet.
- *Education, Entertainment and Leisure* - games, multimedia, etc.

Note that Word Processing and Desktop Publishing head the list. Millions of PCs are equipped with sophisticated packages capable of a far more creative use than just letters and sales reports!

Ironically, despite the electronic revolution, the paperless society is not yet with us and the use of paper-based forms of communication are greater than ever and continue to increase with no sign of decline. Just look at the number and sheer diversity of newspapers, magazines and books currently on offer!

We are not trying to preach to publishing professionals; their art and craft is very specialised and it takes more than a few days practise with a PC and a DTP package to enter their world. However, having successfully published our own books, we can give advice to those with little or no experience of publishing who might also like to publish for themselves. Those readers who have some familiarity with PCs (or those who have not but have the will-power to use one) should find little difficulty in mastering the techniques that we describe.

 | **No Experience of Computers? Don't be daunted!**

For readers who might be interested in publishing, but are not familiar with the use of a PC, do not be put off. Have a go, or at least consider it. Modern desktop publishing software (the programs inside the computers as opposed to hardware which is the physical equipment), is not difficult to learn or use and has become increasingly 'user friendly'. These programs are becoming increasingly intuitive, that is, many of the everyday functions that we use to create documents are anticipated or can be performed with ease, e.g. automatic correction of commonly mistyped words and complete reformatting of a document in a style of your choice. If you already have, or could master some basic keyboard typing skills through practice or even by attending an evening class, you should have little difficulty in using a PC.

1.6   Marketing ....and the Internet

Quite the most challenging aspect of the whole publishing process is being able to sell your products effectively. We will be discussing some conventional marketing methods for books later, with special attention being given to using the Internet.

This new resource is growing at a phenomenal rate and its importance should not be underestimated. It has created a world-wide market that has added an extra dimension to any marketing strategy - and not just in the business of publishing. Even if you are not already using the Internet, you are sure to have heard of its existence. Dubbed by the press as the 'Information Superhighway', it has been alternatively hyped and derided *but,* it is, nonetheless, an immensely significant development in communications on many scales. (Most of the major Daily Newspapers now publish electronic versions on the Internet - such is their concern at being left behind).

Once the preserve of the military, then academic institutions and other large organisations, the Internet is now accessible world-wide and almost universally available in all developed and many developing countries. It is used by a wide range of organisations, companies and individuals. Besides its use for the transmission of electronic mail (e-mail), and connecting groups of far-flung individuals, it provides connections to a *vast* store of diverse information readily accessible to anyone with a telephone socket, modem and PC.

1.6.1 *World Wide Web (www)*

The most significant development in the past few years has been the creation and continuing growth of the 'World Wide Web'. It comprises information held on pages of text, graphics and 'hypertext links'. By accessing a web page, the user can view this information in the manner of conventional book or pamphlet pages. By pointing and 'clicking' (with a mouse) on 'hypertext links' which are highlighted references to other material, the user is carried from one page to another - perhaps to different continents - a process which is sometimes described as 'surfing'.

Web pages are owned and maintained by individuals, organisations of all description, companies, corporations and governments. Even the British Royal family and the Vatican now have their own web site!) They are held on computers known as servers which are located in thousands of places around the world. The vast majority are accessible to you and anyone connected to the Internet. If you are able to create your own web pages with a précis of your book giving some example text and ordering details, then these can be viewed by potential buyers - anywhere in the world.

In a later chapter, we describe how to create your own web page for minimal cost and thereby establish your presence on the Internet. Your web page will be accessible by any of the 40 million+ users world-wide. We cannot overstate the significance of this development and the potential it gives to both individuals and organisations alike. The number of web pages available for view is currently growing at a rate of 8% *per month*.

1.7 Printing Methods

Before you can communicate your creativity to the world, there is the small matter of producing your book! Here we describe three basic methods for the physical production of a book or other publication. The one(s) that you choose to employ will depend upon the scope and nature of your intended project, the volume of production ...and initially, at least, how much you can afford to put into your venture. Starting with the lowest cost method and working forwards from there, we outline the *least risk* route - one that will allow you to expand production in line with the size and demands of your level of sales.

Three methods are suggested:

1) Photocopy Method : Low Volume - Reasonable Quality
For this method you need to produce a high quality 'master copy' of your document on your own or borrowed printer, preferably printed on both sides of the paper. Production is achieved by producing high quality, double-sided photocopies of the document that are bound with covers to form your publication. A local printer or print bureau will be able to produce the covers for you and arrange for binding. The same bureau may also be able to offer competitive rates for photocopying.

2) Laser Printing: Low Volume - High Quality
Instead of photocopying from a master copy, all your copies can be produced on a good quality laser printer and then bound with covers as in 1). If you do not own or have access to such a printer, it may be possible to use a bureau for laser printing. If you do not have a printer capable of printing on both sides of the paper (duplex), the same result can be achieved by reversing the paper after printing on one side and re-printing on the other.

3) High Volume - Highest Quality
This is the conventional print-run usually employing a form of 'off-set litho' printing machine. A print bureau or print shop makes 'plates' of your book and uses them for a print-run. They can also arrange production of the covers and arrange for binding, i.e. handle the entire manufacturing process.

Other than the cost of a laser or inkjet printer, methods 1) and 2) require no set-up costs and will ideally suit those new to self-publishing - but they do have the highest unit cost (for photocopying 3 - 5p per side at the time of writing).

Method 3) is the ideal for high volume production. The initial set-up charge and print run can be high, probably into £1000s depending on various factors including: the size of your book, whether the contents have to be retyped by a typesetter, the quality of the paper used, etc. However, once set up, for volume production, the unit costs come tumbling down! (Typically, 1p or less per side). By reducing your unit costs, naturally you can increase your profit margin.

Low Volume / High Volume?

These are subjective terms. Methods 1) and 2) are most suited to high value, specialist information publications where production can be adjusted to meet demand. We would suggest *low volume* falls into the range of 1-30 copies per week. If your sales are much higher, then small batch runs in which you might produce 25 copies per batch can become rather a chore and you will be missing out on the economies of scale. Method 3), the conventional printing route, requires considerable investment up-front and is best suited to print runs of over 1000 copies. So in our terms, *high volume* refers to batches of 1000+ copies (although minuscule by conventional publishers' standards).

The method that you choose will depend upon a number of factors. Whilst the third option gives you the lowest unit production cost, it does require the highest initial outlay and you will be taking delivery of a considerable quantity of stock. If you are unable to sell this stock through your marketing endeavours, your spare bedroom, loft, garage or wherever, may be taken up for some considerable time. Remember also, that paper is not very tolerant of damp and other adverse conditions so your investment will need to be protected from the elements!

> **Tip:** A successful production strategy that we have used is a progression through methods 1), 2) and 3). Method 1) for a 'toe in the water', method 2) self-financing of better equipment through sales and finally 3) self-financing and confidence that we will be able to sell our stock, thereby taking advantage of lower unit costs and reduced demands on our time and labour.

2. The Tools You Need

2.1 Hardware

You will need a Personal Computer (PC) and related equipment to create an electronic document that, when completed, will form your manuscript for publication. You could, of course, work in longhand with pen and ink and arrange for someone else to do the preparatory work on the document using their equipment. This, however, to a large extent, removes the 'satisfaction' factor from the enterprise. Self-reliance is a major theme running through this book so we will proceed with the assumption that you, as both author and publisher, will be doing as much of the work as you are able on your own or loaned equipment.

The most practical approach is to create a document, or documents on a PC. The most suitable form will be either an IBM[T] PC compatible computer, or on Apple[T] equipment. The cost of these has been steadily falling over the past few years and acquiring one suitable for a publishing project is well within reach of most people. There is a burgeoning market in PC 'clones' - independent manufacturers who assemble equipment from industry-standard components. Also, many second-hand bargains are now to be had as people and companies upgrade to new more powerful systems. If you already have a PC, and are familiar with basic functions such as word processing and spreadsheets, you will be able to skip most of this section - you are already at an advantage.

Virtually all PCs sold from new are now capable of running the sort of DTP package that you will need to produce a professional looking document. However, it is worth remembering that if you are going to be spending a lot of time 'at the keyboard', there are a few considerations that either make your task easier, faster or more comfortable.

2.1.1 Your PC

A standard off-the-shelf PC package comprises several separate parts:

- 📖 A base unit, containing processor(s), memory, disk drives and maybe optional devices such as CD drives, tape back-up, etc.
- 📖 A monitor or VDU (visual display unit) which enables you to view your work in progress.
- 📖 A keyboard for typing.
- 📖 ..and a mouse that is used to point and click in your window's environment.

You can obtain a PC from many sources: High Street shops, specialist distributors or direct from the manufacturer. One of the many personal computer magazines will give you an idea of suppliers and prices. A PC usually comes with all the components listed above, plus perhaps some optional extras. Most product lines start with a 'base' configuration and progressively increase in price as options are added. As with buying a car, choosing which one to buy can be a difficult process - largely because of the enormous choice available and the technological knowledge needed to determine the specifications required. Weighing up the relative price/ performance/ features options can require much evaluation, especially as some suppliers will bundle in software packages that may or may not be of particular value to you. Do think about what will be the main use(s) of your PC and do a little research on the sort of specification you will need. We strongly urge you not just to visit a High Street store and buy a machine on impulse - you are likely to pay much more than if you shopped around.

To obtain the equipment specification that best suits your needs, draw up a shopping list beforehand. If we use buying a car as an analogy: travelling from point A to point B, if you intend to travel no faster than 30 mph it is immaterial whether you know the engine is fuel injected, has 16 valves or a turbo-charger. If you are taking the children to school, however, it would be more practical to use an estate car than a sports model - so do try and refine your requirements before you buy. If you are specifically basing your choice on 'Desk Top Publishing' requirements, the following sections may be helpful.

2.1.2 Computer jargon

If you are not familiar with the jargon that unfortunately surrounds computers, do not worry. Even computer aficionados probably do not fully understand the meanings of the terminology that are in common use. There is no mystique: you will be using a glorified typewriter - no more, no less - and only a basic understanding of its construction is needed.

2.1.3 *The base unit*

We would say that the following specification is about the minimum you should consider. You can get by with less, but your progress is better limited by your imagination than the tools you use to exercise it! In reality, unless you buy second-hand, you will find it difficult to buy *below* these specifications.

Processor speed

Processor speed determines the rate which many computing functions are performed. Speed is measured in Megahertz (MHz) which is a meaningless measurement to most people. A 66Mhz or faster Intel or equivalent 486 - type CPU (Central Processing Unit) is required. In reality, most new PCs sold are the much faster Pentium-based machines. For most DTP functions, however, the processor speed is not necessarily the limiting factor and the processing power of virtually all current PC models (usually over 120MHz) should be quite adequate.

Memory

When you are working on a document, as much of it as possible will be loaded into your PC's 'dynamic' memory. This includes the DTP program itself, text and images, etc. Editing the document when it is held in memory, is very fast and efficient. However, if your document is very large, only part of it can reside entirely within memory. The rest will remain on disk and will be moved in and out of memory as required from the computer's disk drive. This can become irritating as, although it is tolerable for a while, it is much slower. Even waiting for a few extra seconds becomes irksome, especially when you move backwards and forwards through large documents. 8Mb of memory is the minimum you should aspire to (1 Megabytes, or Mb = 1 million bytes of information). 16Mb is better and 32Mb ideal. The cost of extra memory has been falling rapidly so go for as much as you can afford. [Note that Microsoft Windows 95 will run on 8Mb but is more effective with 16Mb or more]. The more you have, the smoother the DTP program will run.

Hard Disk Capacity

Your hard disk will be where your PC permanently stores its operating system (Windows 3.x, 95, etc.), program packages, data and your document(s). No less than 500Mb size disk is recommended. It is surprising how quickly you can use up this kind of capacity. A typical DTP Package and several copies of a typical 200 page book, plus other related materials, are together likely to exceed 250Mb of disk storage. There are utility programs to double the apparent capacity of the disk so 340Mb becomes perhaps equivalent of 600Mb or more. Like the cost of memory, hard disk costs have been falling and very few base level machines are now sold with less than 500Mb. The cost of another 500Mb might only be another £40 or so on top of the basic entry price ...it's well worth it if you can afford it. Note that most new machines now are sold with at least 1Gb (1 gigabyte = 1000Mb).

> **Tip**: Buy as much memory and disk space as you can afford. It is cheaper and more convenient to obtain a higher specification when you buy your equipment than it is to upgrade later.

Graphics card with 1Mb is normally adequate for most DTP functions using a standard 14" monitor. The card and its memory will affect the speed at which your monitor will refresh and the number of colours and resolution it will support. Note that larger monitors may require 2Mb or more to provide the high resolution required.

Optional Accessories for the Base Unit - Not essential but useful:

CD ROM

CDs (compact discs) are the preferred media for software distribution as well as a host of other applications including games and entertainment packages. Much reference material is now available on CD including 'clip art' and other image libraries; these can be useful for illustration purposes. When a sound card and speakers are added to CD ROM it is known as 'multi-media'. [CD ROM drives together with a sound card will allow you to play your music CDs whilst you are working on the PC ....which you may find inspirational!]

Tape Back-up

As we will reiterate, it is good practice to take copies of your documents on a regular basis. If your PC breaks down, is stolen or damaged, it will be essential for you to restore your work, maybe onto another machine. An alternative to making floppy disk copies is to back-up your files to a magnetic tape drive that takes cassette style tapes. One of these tapes can store up to 800Mb or more of disk files whereas a standard 3.5" floppy disk can only store 1.35Mb. A tape drive is therefore a good investment; they start at about £75 in price.

External Disk Drive

A good alternative to a tape back-up device is an external removable disk drive. This device, not much bigger than a portable CD player, plugs into the back of your PC's parallel port (into which a printer is normally plugged). Popular makes take 25Mb or 100Mb diskettes that are not much bigger than a normal 3.5" floppy disk. The drive itself is configured on the PC (or Apple Mac) as a separate disk drive. Unlike a magnetic tape drive, the external disk drive operates at much the same speed as a CD ROM and may be used in much the same way as a hard disk drive. Copies of important files can be copied on to diskettes that can then be stored safely and easily re-read. Prices currently start at about £120 + £10 each for the diskettes. Higher capacity devices are available but at greater cost.

2.1.4 The monitor

Remember that you will be sitting staring at your monitor for many hours (more than you would care to estimate, or admit to, anyway). It is worthwhile, therefore, if you are going to buy a new one, making the right choice (more so, maybe than when you buy a new television set). The standard size is 14" across the diagonal but in reality, the viewing area will be slightly less than this as there is usually  a dark border around the viewing area of varying size. The viewing size is usually adjustable but there is normally an optimum height to width aspect ratio that gives the best appearance and resolution. Probably for another £50-60 you can have a 15" monitor that will, to some, make a difference. Better still is a 17" monitor and, if you are not constrained by finances, a 21" may be the best solution. Note however, 14" & 15" monitors fit reasonably well onto a standard work desk whereas 17" and 21" monitors are real monsters and take up considerable extra desk space.

More so than other applications such as spreadsheets, accountancy packages, databases, etc., working with Desk Top Publishing (DTP) greatly benefits from use of the larger monitor sizes. At certain stages, it is easier to view your creations a full page at a time. The aspect ratios of monitors and book pages are generally diametrically opposite. Books tend to be in 'portrait' mode (height is greater than width) whereas most monitors are in 'landscape' mode (width greater than height). A standard 14" monitor does not allow you to view an entire full size A4 page in portrait mode. You can squeeze a whole A4 page by reducing its magnification; it will, however, be on the verge of legibility but if you have a larger screen legibility improves. This factor does not in reality limit you as you can 'scroll' your pages up and down on the screen but, if you can afford it, consider a screen bigger than the standard 14", especially if you have poor eyesight or suffer from eye strain. It is possible to buy monitors that have a portrait mode aspect ratio (taller than wide) but these are much more expensive than normal monitors. *Note that this book was compiled using a 14" screen - but we have used the A5 format. You can quite comfortably view two adjacent A5 pages on a 14" monitor in portrait mode.*

What you see on a 14" monitor using a 75% magnification of an A4 size page viewing area:

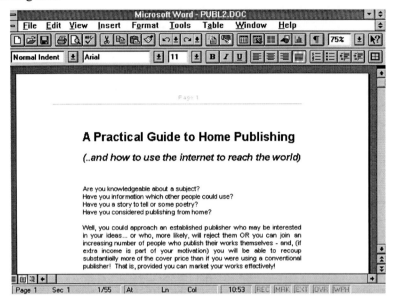

...and viewing two whole adjacent pages of A5 with a 14" monitor - not ideal but legible when viewed on the screen and adequate for seeing the effect of a layout.

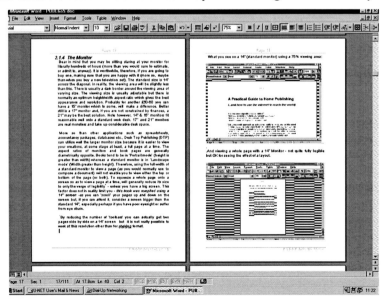

2.1.5 Health Aspects

Much concern has been expressed about the effects on health of prolonged use of computers, particularly with regard to monitors. Virtually all monitors manufactured nowadays have to comply with rigorous standards for emission of electromagnetic radiation. The US Environment Protection Agency has very stringent rules and most manufacturers adhere to them. Correct lighting, good seating posture and adequate rest periods all contribute to sensible use of your PC that should not normally have any detrimental effects on health. However, if you are prone to eye strain and/or headaches, then particular care should be taken when choosing your monitor. Women who are pregnant are also advised not to spend prolonged periods using a PC. If you are concerned about this, then it would be worth contacting The Health and Safety Executive for specialist advice.

2.1.6 Keyboard and mouse

Keyboards are also a matter of personal preference;  some have a quiet soft touch while others are 'rattly' and 'clicky'. The keyboard supplied as standard should suffice but if you are particular (as we are) then try it out. If you tend to work late into the night, and have children who are light sleepers then a quiet keyboard might be advantageous!

The mouse is a pointing device that allows you to click (select) on words, icons, etc. It is essential for working in a Windows environment. Many of the word processing features you will need use the mouse. Some mice are regarded as more 'ergonomic'(and are more expensive). The one provided with a standard PC will probably be adequate.

2.1.7 Laptops & Notebook PCs vs. Desk Top PCs

Laptop and Notebook PCs, weighing only a few pounds, are becoming increasingly popular and offer complete portability, i.e. the freedom to travel. What could be more ideal than composing your *opus magnum* on holiday, sitting on the beach, or using time on the train, lunchbreaks, etc.?  These machines are now very powerful and carry the same level of specification as conventional desktop PCs - at a price. Be prepared to pay up to double the price for a laptop with the same specifications as a desktop model. Also, note that, whilst peripherals such as scanners and modems can be attached, the miniaturised versions of the interfaces are generally much more expensive than the desktop equivalent. If you think a laptop PC will suit you best and money is not really a problem, these other points should be considered:

Advantages

- 📖 Portability, take and use anywhere.
- 📖 Space saving; can be kept in a drawer or briefcase - no need to allocate permanent living space!

Disadvantages

- 📖 Batteries still only have a limited life. Away from the mains, you will get 2 - 6 hour's life out of a fully charged power unit (depending on model).
- 📖 Screen size is smaller: typically 9.5"- 10.5" diagonal which is not quite so comfortable for hours and hours of viewing.
- 📖 Keyboard: because miniaturisation has been the driving force for these machines, the keyboard will usually be smaller and more awkward to use. You do become used to this in time - but some keyboards are definitely more ergonomic than others.
- 📖 Price: As previously mentioned, a well-featured machine will cost you a lot more than a desk top equivalent. (At the time of writing you will need to pay £1100+ for a good colour Notebook with an Intel Pentium processor, 16Mb RAM and 500Mb+ of disk space.)

Docking Stations

It is possible to have the best of both worlds by using a 'docking station'. This is a desk bound device into which your notebook or laptop is plugged. It can then take on the characteristics of a normal desktop PC as the laptop can be connected to a conventional monitor, keyboard and other types of peripheral.

2.2   Printer - Generalities

The type of printer you will require will depend on which process you use to publish your work. As far as quality is concerned, the excellence and precision of modern printers are a marvel to behold. Great strides in printing technology have been made in the past few years. It is unlikely you will be disappointed with any of the modern printers currently on sale. The brand leaders are Hewlett-Packard and Canon who are the pace-setters and produce both laser and ink/bubblejet printers. There are, however, a number of other manufacturers who provide a range of alternatives.

We will be discussing the options for the actual means of printing copies of your book later. For the moment, we will assume that you would like to purchase a printer that prints text and graphics in as high a quality as you can afford.

You should be looking for a printer that produces clear and crisp text and graphics at least to a resolution of 300dpi (dots per inch). Most contemporary printers will better this, few being rated at less than 600x600dpi. There are two types to consider:

- 📖 Inkjet/ Bubblejet
- 📖 Laser (or LED)

2.2.1 Inkjet/ bubblejet printers

These are the low cost alternatives to laser printers. Prices currently range from about £120 to over £500. For £200+ you will get a superb printer, capable of printing at least to 360x360dpi if not higher. Most manufacturers claim resolutions of 360x720 or 600x600dpi - on best quality paper. It is more than likely that at this price the printer will print in colour too (although this is of limited use for publishing purposes).

These printers work by heating up small amounts of ink that expand rapidly causing it to be squirted selectively through a minute array of nozzles. A print-head moves in proximity to the sheet of paper squirting ink in the desired pattern. The resolution is not quite that of a quality laser printer, but it is very close.

Running costs: There are few moving parts to wear out and the print-head is usually replaced when the cartridge is empty. Monochrome cartridges generally last for between 100 and 300 pages (standard quality), longer in draft mode. The unit cost of printing (ink) per page is, however, comparatively high at 3 - 6p per page. Many cartridges, however, can be refilled using kits that will bring the cost down substantially. Colour cartridges are more expensive, printing in colour typically costs 10-15p per page.

Advantages:
- 📖 About £100 less than the cheapest lasers for (almost) the same high quality print.
- 📖 Small, quiet.
- 📖 Can print on a variety of paper materials (paper and card).
- 📖 Can usually print colour.

Disadvantages:
- 📖 Higher per unit printing costs than a laser.
- 📖 Quality generally very good but not quite as good as a laser.
- 📖 For best results, good quality paper is required which is more expensive. The ink tends to 'run' slightly on poorer quality paper.

    📖 Not suited to high volume output as they average only 2-3ppm (pages per minute).

    📖 The inks used are not waterproof so books should not be produced directly from this kind of printer.

Only the best of this type of printer is able to produce good greyscales; greys (as opposed to solid black) are produced using faint hatching and stippling. Note that these may not photocopy very well so, if you intend to use a photocopy process, test any output of this form in advance.

2.2.2 Laser printers

Laser printers will, on balance, give you the best quality output combined with lower running costs. Colour printers are available but very expensive. Lasers are generally rated for higher volumes of printing (typically 2,000-20,000 pages per month). Unlike inkjets and bubblejets, which use liquid ink, lasers  use fine toner powder that is 'welded' to the page using heat in a similar manner to a photocopier. Laser print quality is less susceptible to paper types as it does not suffer so badly when using cheaper, more fibrous, paper.

Print Resolution and Speed

For a modern 300dpi printer, laser prices start at about £200. At this price you can expect 3-4 ppm (pages per minute). A 600dpi laser is only slightly more expensive, starting at the low end around £230. Prices increase with extra features and print speed. An 'office duty' printer, capable of producing many thousands of prints per month with speed of 10-12 ppm currently costs around £850.

Memory Requirement

Most lasers rely on the PC building a 'bit map' of the image to be printed; the image is computed and then transmitted to the laser. Where a page contains large photographs or elaborate graphics, more memory is required in the printer than for just plain text. If you intend to use a lot of graphics, check with the supplier for the appropriate amount of memory that you are likely to require for your laser. As a rule of thumb, avoid buying a laser with less than 1Mb of memory fitted.

GDI Lasers

There is a category of laser printers on the market that are cheaper because they contain simplified electronics. Instead of using its own memory and bit map processing, a GDI (Graphical Device Interface) printer uses the power of the PC to create the 'bit-map' to be output. Therefore, the faster your PC works, the faster the printing will be (to the maximum rating of the printer). They produce excellent quality output for low cost but can be a drain on your PC's CPU resources if you intend to do a lot of printing while concurrently working on your document. They are not suitable for the slower PCs (<66Mhz) and some will only work in a Windows environment.

Duplex Printing

Some 'high end' printers have an optional 'duplex' unit. In this context, duplex means printing on both sides of each sheet of paper. If you are considering using a laser directly to produce pages for your books (an option if you are anticipating relatively low numbers of sales), then duplex printing may be the best solution for your printing needs. A duplex unit which reverses the paper after printing the first side, normally sits below the main body of the printer and is purchased separately. The current cost of a duplex add-on unit is typically £350-£400 extra to the standard printer price.

Printer Protocols: PostScript vs. PCL

In 1985 the Adobe company came up with a page description language called PostScript (Level 1). This is a device-independent printer language that uses a 'vectoring' technique. A document prepared for a postscript printer will appear in the same format however the actual postscript-compatible printer is employed. It is used primarily by 'high end' applications (N.B. standard on Apple) and is almost standard within the publishing industry. Thus, if you prepare your document on a lower specification printer at home, you may be able to create a 'print-file' that can be printed on your local print bureau's fast, high resolution machine or even have it transferred to a photo-print process. PostScript printers tend to be more expensive (typically £100+ more than non-PostScript equivalents) as they require a specialised processor to translate PostScript commands into bitmapped images. Meanwhile, Hewlett-Packard devised their own page description language called PCL (Print Command Language) which has been widely cloned by other printer manufacturers. Unfortunately, although a printer may be described as PCL (usually II or III) compatible, the printer drivers are device-specific so 'print-files' may only be transportable between printers in the same product range. PCL compatible printers are the more widespread and are cheaper than PostScript printers.

32

Bargain Hunting
It is possible to pick up end-of-line bargains costing £150+ for less advanced technology (i.e. they use more energy and toner, are slower or do not print to the same resolution). Do check the future availability of toner and replacement components.

Running Costs
The cost of replacing a spent toner cartridge may seem expensive (£50-£110) but it is likely to last for 3000-6000 pages of output (1-2p per sheet). When choosing a laser, check the costs of toner cartridges and other parts that are likely to need renewing. Note that toner is likely to be the most expensive factor in laser bulk printing.

Advantages of lasers over ink/ bubblejet printers:
- Cheaper to run, approx. 3000-6000 sheets per toner cartridge.
- Highest quality.
- Less fussy about paper quality so cheaper paper can be used.
- Higher throughput, 4-24ppm depending on printer and page content.
- Available with PostScript compatibility.

Disadvantages:
- Higher initial cost.
- Colour not really an option yet.
- Some of the older (non-GDI) printers require more memory to cope with large images and other graphics - extra memory can be quite expensive.

Conclusion
Horses for courses! You should not be disappointed with either a modern laser or bubble/inkjet printer. Both types will give you excellent results. If your budget is tight and you only anticipate (on average) relatively low volume printing and the occasional use of colour, an ink or bubblejet should be adequate for your purposes. [You could follow our 'method 1' route and use a bubble/inkjet to produce a master copy for photocopying.] For higher volume work and top quality - go for a laser printer, especially if you are considering producing your books directly on your own printer. If you can afford one, buy a PostScript compatible printer as it will give you greater flexibility.

For your project, it might be worth using a cheap printer for draft copies and borrow a better one for higher quality. Alternatively, produce print files on floppy disks to be printed on higher quality equipment somewhere else (work, college, local business, Printers, etc.) But beware, as has been mentioned, unless using PostScript, each type of printer has its own particular 'driver'- a piece of software that is used to translate your document into actual print commands. Font & page sizes DO differ slightly and may cause your nicely arranged page formats to go awry when the number of lines per page changes!

Check carefully for added-value software included with a printer. For example, some printers, particularly PostScript and high-end printers may include extra fonts and advanced formatting programs. You may find that your DTP package does not include the ability to create 'Booklets' but your printer may come with add-on software to provide this feature (see Booklet Printing).

Tip: To produce a print file that can be printed on another PC's printer, take a copy of your document, select the appropriate printer type in the printer set-up section of your DTP. Make it the default. Correct any formatting changes. When you have a document you want printed, write to a file instead of the printer (see how to do this using the set-up). The resultant print files can be transferred (i.e. by floppy disk) to another PC and printer for printing.

2.2.3 Image and OCR scanners

Reproducing Images
You may not be able to create all the illustrations you require by solely using the capabilities of your DTP. For example, in this particular book, there are a number of illustrations either hand-drawn or from other sources. The method by which a diagram, photograph or other picture is 'captured' into a document is via an image scanner. A scanner is a device that transforms images into a computer readable format (bitmapped) from where they can be stored in disk files to be imported into documents. The resolution at which images are captured, like printer quality, is measured in dots per inch (dpi). A monochrome diagram, such as a line drawing will reproduce well at 300dpi but photographs and other textured pictures require much higher resolutions to be effective. Most reasonably priced scanners work in the range of 400-1200dpi. *Note, however, that reproduction of images is more likely to be limited by the resolution capability of your printer than your scanner .*

Scanners work much like a facsimile machine; indeed, combined scanners/ fax/ printers are available - but at a cost. The price range is considerable but, if you want to reproduce only small images in black & white, you should be satisfied with a device for less than £75.

OCR: Scanning text into a document

When you buy a scanner, the price will include a 'bundle' of software that enables you to create, edit and manipulate scanned images. An Optical Character Recognition (OCR) package is often included with the imaging software. This may be very useful to the author/ publisher as it is used to read scanned text from a page and turn it into text that can be pasted into your DTP document. This facility could be invaluable if a manuscript has been typed on a conventional typewriter or is already in a report or book - it can save having to retype the text. OCR programs are now very good but not perfect so you must expect some errors in the translation. Nonetheless, it could still be a boon. *A note of caution: do be careful about breeches of copyright.*

There are various file formats in which images can be stored and they are denoted by the 'file extensions' that suffix the file name (.tif, .gif, .bmp, etc.). Most commonly, you will need a .tif file for importing into your document and a .gif file for an Internet web page. It is worth checking that the software that is supplied with a scanner is capable of creating both formats.

Note, that whilst the quality of reproduction for diagrams and black on white line drawings can be superb, obtaining a good replication of a photograph by this means is not easy unless you have high resolution equipment. You will need both scanner and printer rated at 600dpi+. There are two main types of scanner to consider: hand-held and desk-top. Of the latter type, there are two kinds, flat-bed scanners and document scanners.

Many scanners come with a controller card that slots into your PC so you may need a free slot on your PC's motherboard. Some devices, however, can be plugged directly into the parallel port at the rear of the PC. This latter type does not need a controller card but is often more costly and tends to be rather slower in operation.

Hand Held Scanners

These are generally designed for occasional use and are the lowest cost option. They are hand-held T-shaped devices with a scan head 4-5" wide. The user pulls the scan head over the required image, keeping contact with the paper. Scanning area dimensions are pre-set by the user so that the device ceases to scan after the required area has been covered. Small rubber rollers on the underside assist in keeping to a straight line but some practice is needed to get a steady image and to find the right settings for sensitivity and contrast. A maximum scan size of about 5"x12" is achievable using a hand scanner but images can be 'stitched' together if larger images are required. In practice, this is rather tiresome and can result in less than satisfactory results. The software provided will allow you to edit the image (clean it up, change the density and contrast, crop it, rotate the image, etc.).

Prices

Most hand scanners sold now will scan both colour and black and white. They come with the necessary leads, controller cards and software. Prices range from under £75 to about £150. If cost is an issue, black and white only scanners can be purchased for as little as £50.

Advantages of hand scanners

- 📖 Small, portable and will probably scan in the majority of images you will want to use.
- 📖 Inexpensive.

Disadvantages

- 📖 Scanning in graphs or illustrations with 'dead-straight' lines can be frustrating! Needs practise to get accurate images.
- 📖 Image capture limit of about 4.5" wide images (but 'stitching' can be done for larger pictures).
- 📖 Can be frustrating if there is a lot of scanning to do as several attempts may be needed for each capture to get a good 'take'.
- 📖 If you intend to use the OCR facility to scan and translate text, the maximum scan width may not be sufficiently wide to accommodate the text you wish to read.

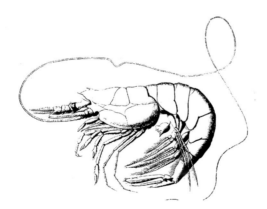

The above illustration of a deep-sea shrimp, and all the other scanned images in this book were captured using an inexpensive hand-held scanner. Note: *Do be aware of copyright infringements! You may need to ask permission from the original author or publisher if you want to reproduce their work in your own publication.*

Flatbed Scanners

A flatbed scanner is rather a like a small photocopier. The picture to be scanned is placed over a glass window and a scan head automatically travels the length of the image under the glass window. This type is easy to use and will produce results of a consistent  quality but can cost considerably more than hand-held scanners. Prices for colour scanners start at about £145 but rise rapidly with specification. The best models (for speed and resolution) exceed £750. Most flatbed scanners are A4 format enabling scanning of images up to 210x297mm. Recently, A5 format versions have been appearing (max. image 148x210mm) which are ideal for most photographs. These smaller machines also have the advantage of taking up only a small amount of desk space.

Note: Image manipulation becomes progressively processor and memory-intensive with increased image size and resolution. If you have much scanning to do, you will find a basic 66Mhz, 8Mb specified PC very frustrating to use! We would suggest that a Pentium processor with at least 16Mb of RAM, would be the minimum specification if there are more than just a few small images to be processed.

Advantages of a flatbed scanner
- Produces images of consistent high quality.
- Generally higher resolution than hand-held devices.
- Will cope with pictures and diagrams up to A4 in size.
- For OCR purposes this type should be adequate for most sources of text.
- Faster and more convenient to operate.

Disadvantages
- More expensive.
- Takes up more desk space - similar 'footprint' to a laser printer (though consider the smaller A5 variety).

Document Scanners

As the name implies, this type of scanner is intended primarily for translating external documents into usable text for incorporating into your own documents. They function much like a facsimile machine with a document sheet being drawn into and passed out of the machine through rubber rollers. Similarly, some document scanners will allow you to process a number of pages rather than feed them in individually. They can be used for image capture but usually offer a lower degree of resolution than a flatbed scanner. Most are for monochrome work but some will process colour. They require the source material on separate sheets of paper, like a fax machine, so would not be much use for copying images in books or other bound documents. Prices start at about £120.

Advantages of a document scanner

📖 Ideal if you want to translate a number of typed pages into your word processor.

📖 Automatic feed - does not need practise to use like a hand scanner.

📖 Comparatively inexpensive compared to a flatbed scanner.

📖 Small and compact, taking much less space than a flatbed scanner.

Disadvantages

📖 Tend to be lower resolution than flatbed scanners (150-300dpi).

📖 Require source material to be on sheets of paper.

Conclusions

As with printers previously discussed, consider what is best suited to your particular needs. If you wish to incorporate say, small (up to 3"x3") hand-drawn or other images into your document, then a hand scanner will probably be perfectly adequate. If you are going to require many images, especially if they are large and require high quality reproduction or have dead straight lines then a flatbed scanner will be required. If you need a scanner primarily for importing printed text on loose sheets into DTP documents, then consider a document scanner. There is another option, if you only have occasional need of a scanner, then why not get your diagrams and illustrations scanned at work, college, at a print bureau, friends, etc. and bring your .tif files (or whatever) home on a floppy disk!

2.2.4 Modems

A modem (short for **mod**ulator **dem**odulator) is a communications device for connecting your PC to other computers via the telephone network. It sits between your PC and the telephone socket and converts your computer's signal into one that can be transmitted by telephony. A modem at the other end reverses this process. When overheard with a telephone ear-piece, the dialogue between computers sounds rather like the shriek of a fax machine. You will need a modem if you want to use the Internet or if you want to exchange files with someone with whom you are collaborating.

There are several things to consider. If you are unfamiliar with modems, choosing one is rather bewildering - there are many conventions and technical terms. However, the issues you are faced with are simple. All modems sold these days come with sophisticated specifications (data compression, adherence to various standards, error checking, etc.) but SPEED is the most important factor. The faster the modem is capable of transmitting and receiving data, the shorter the time you need to be connected to an Internet service or a colleague's computer over the telephone network and the cheaper your phone bill will be. Avoid buying a modem with a transmission speed of less then 14,400bps (bits per second). A good quality 14.4k device will cost £50-£80 but, if you can afford to spend more, buy a model capable of 28.8k bps or faster for £60-£150, depending on the features offered. You should get some software included such as a fax emulator (which enables you to use your PC to send and receive faxes) and maybe free subscription for a limited period to an Internet provider. The other distinct advantage of a higher speed modem is the shorter time it takes to down-load 'web' pages. These frequently contain a high proportion of data-intensive images so the faster your modem, the quicker the images arrive. Waiting for a picture arriving on your monitor, line by line is about as interesting as watching paint dry!

Installing a modem is usually a very simple operation, especially if your computer's operating system has a 'plug and play' facility (e.g. Windows 95). In this case, your computer will perform most of the installing tasks for you without your intervention.

Internal vs. External Modems
An internal modem fits inside your PC and slots onto the motherboard (another slot taken!). The only external wiring visible is the cable that plugs into the telephone socket. External modems are small boxes the size of a portable CD player or smaller. Although some are battery powered most require a main's electricity supply; they plug into the back of your PC (COM2 port usually) and into the telephone socket. There is a bit more clutter involved with these BUT they do have little lights on them that flash reassuringly when everything is working normally. If you are having problems connecting and communicating with, say, your Internet service, the lights on the front of an external modem will give you a clue to what is going on! External modems are also very portable and can easily be moved from PC to PC - useful if you need to lend or borrow one. Another advantage of an external modem is protection. In the event of a lightning strike, telephone lines connected directly into your PC and attached to a modem card, could result in extensive damage to the PC's motherboard. An external modem does give a greater level of protection as it does not connect directly into the motherboard and so limits the damage.

2.2.5 Conclusions for computer hardware
So what exactly will you need to kit yourself out for DTP work? There are enormous variations in hardware specifications and prices. As with other conventional tools, you normally "get what you pay for". Professionally rated equipment commands premium prices but there are often cheaper equivalents. The cheaper variants may not be the choice of industry professionals but they

should be perfectly acceptable for a small-scale or start-up enterprise for which budgets might be limited. The equipment used to prepare and publish this book was all 'basic' priced. All of it is readily available from High Street stores or by mail-order. Below we detail three typical set-ups, budget, basic and, in our opinion, 'deluxe'.

Budget

Item	Description	Price (£ approx.)
PC	486DX4 100Mhz with 16MB RAM & 850Mb Disk' 14" Monitor, x6 speed CDROM	575
Scanner	Hand Scanner 4" Head	50
Printer	Inkjet or Bubblejet	175
Modem	28,800 Internal	60
	Total	**£860**

Basic

Item	Description	Price (£ approx.)
PC	120Mhz Pentium with 16Mb RAM & 1Gb Disk (1000Mb), sound card 14" Monitor and x8 speed CDROM	750
Scanner	A4 Flat Bed Scanner	150
Printer	600dpi, 6ppm Laser	260
Modem	28,800bps Internal	60
	Total	**£1220**

Deluxe

Item	Description	Price (£ approx.)
PC	166Mhz Pentium with 32Mb RAM & 2Gb Disk, sound card, 17" Monitor and x12 speed CDROM	1300
Scanner	A4 Flat Bed Scanner	280
Printer	600dpi, 12ppm Laser with Duplex unit	1250
Modem	33,600bps Internal/External	120
External removable disk drive	100Mb diskettes (or 800Mb tape drive as alternative back-up media)	120
	Total	**£3070**

Prices quoted are for the UK and based on typical direct or mail-order suppliers (early summer 1997). Prices do not include VAT (17.5%).

2.3 Software - Choosing a Desktop Publishing Package

What you will need:

A Good Quality DTP Package.
If you already use a DTP package and are familiar with its features, strengths and weaknesses, then you may decide to skip over this section. However, if you are not completely satisfied with your package, now could be the time to review your requirements. It is advisable not to change packages halfway through a project; one good reason for this is that diagrams created using the drawing features in a DTP package may not easily be converted for use in another package or worse, may need re-drawing.

There are two main types of package to consider:
1) High-end professional publisher's programs such as Pagemaker and QuarkXpress.
2) General purpose office-type programs such as Microsoft Word for Windows, WordPerfect and Lotus WordPro. These last three are the market leaders for professional 'office' packages.

The first type, used throughout the publishing industry, are expensive, specialist and take considerable mastering but will cope with just about any DTP function you are likely to meet. If you have sufficient funds to buy such a package and have the time to master all the advanced features, then this may be the type for you - particularly if you intend to produce a number of publications. However, the theme of this book is just how inexpensive it can be to publish, and so we are concentrating on less expensive and less specialised tools. We will, therefore, focus on the latter class of products.

The 'office' type products may not be as sophisticated as Pagemaker and QuarkXpress, but they are still aimed at the 'professional' user and should not disappoint any but the most discerning user. The market for DTP packages is very competitive and dominated by only a handful of players. As a result, prices are keen, and they do represent excellent value for money. The leading programs, as listed above, are generally excellent and offer a comprehensive set of features. All offer the basic functions but some offer more and each has its foibles! To date, the perfect package has not been created - so it is wise, if you are not already equipped with one, to compare the features between the leading products before embarking on your project. Incidentally, this book has been written using Microsoft's Word 7 for Windows™.

For letters, small reports and documents, it is unlikely that you will find much to tell them apart. However, when working on a major project of any length (say 100pages+), feature differences between packages begin to show.

Here are some features to consider when choosing a package:

Essential Features:

- 📖 Drag & drop editing. (Highlight an area of text and 'drag' it to a new location).
- 📖 Spell Checker (preferably with a UK dictionary - if for the UK!).
- 📖 Thesaurus (very handy when you are stuck for alternative words).
- 📖 Ability to open many files concurrently (thus enabling cut and paste between documents).
- 📖 Ability to import external objects, e.g. graphics files and text from other packages.
- 📖 Ability to move diagrams and images around the page as well as control the flow of text surrounding them.
- 📖 Ability to use 'icons' for the most commonly used operations and be able to adjust them for preference.
- 📖 Ability to generate a Table of Contents (TOC) and an Index.
- 📖 Ability to switch automatic document-saving on or off.
- 📖 $^{Supertext} / _{Subtext}$
- 📖 Bullet points & lists.
- 📖 Ability to 'undo'/'redo' last edit to several levels - for correcting mistakes in changes to text, layout, etc.
- 📖 Ability to toggle between modes (draft mode - printer layout mode).
- 📖 Ability to alter the size of view (zoom in / out, full page, facing pages, etc.).
- 📖 Good drawing facilities - for diagrams.
- 📖 Good table facilities (control styles such as borders, cut & paste rows & columns).
- 📖 Ability to anchor graphics to text, i.e. so the diagrams, pictures, etc. stay in the same position relative to the text and do not wander away when text is added or deleted.
- 📖 Ability to break up a large document into smaller parts and 'stitch' them together to look like a single document.

Desirable Features:

- 📖 Ability to manipulate text for special effects (e.g. WordArt in MS Word).
- 📖 Ability to auto-format a document in a selected style (saves much hard work).
- 📖 Import Spreadsheets, parts of databases, etc.
- 📖 Produce merged documents with other objects (databases, spreadsheets).
- 📖 Ability to work with very large files (several Mb).

📖 Provision of comprehensive page formats - i.e. 'Booklet' printing, where multiple pages are printed on a single sheet of paper.

📖 Automatic Spell Checking - i.e. DTP marks what it considers erroneous words just after they have been typed in.

📖 Grammar Checker. (N.B. There may be several levels of rules that can be applied - Business English, for example).

WP vs. DTP: Word Processing was an early development of PC software. Early programs were relatively simple and only capable of handling text and very simple graphics. With time and successive versions, these packages have become much more sophisticated and are now capable of complex font setting, formatting, drawing, picture embedding and page control. Hence, pure word processing programs have all but disappeared. Virtually all former 'word processors' have evolved to include advanced DTP features.

2.4 Other PC Software that the Publisher/ Small Business will Find Useful

Your PC will be invaluable for a number of other applications that will aid you as a small publishing business. Here are a few:

Creating Illustrations
You may not be able to create all the illustrations you need within your normal DTP package. There may be more complicated diagrams and artwork that can be created in specialised graphics packages. Examples are: drawing packages, CAD (Computer Aided Design) and photograph editing. For scientific and technical documents, you may need the services of advanced maths and statistical packages to produce graphs and charts.

'Publishing' Software
There are specialist packages for producing newsletters, brochures, advertisements and labels that a small business may find useful for producing marketing material and office stationery, etc. One such package, Microsoft Publisher can also be used to create web pages. (It also comes complete with over 5,000 clip-art images).

Conducting Correspondence
You will inevitably need to write a great number of letters to: suppliers, customers, colleagues, tax authorities, etc. Your DTP/ word processor will be ideal for this task. All letters sent will be available on file for recall as and when necessary.

Sales and Accounts
You may either use a specialist package to record customer orders, generate invoices, reminders and address labels, etc., or more simply, you may use a spreadsheet to monitor sales and cashflow. At some point, you may be required to submit accounts to an accountant, tax authorities, etc. Summarised accounts output from computerised records will be invaluable.

Marketing
This includes the maintenance of a customer database. Production of mail shot letters by merging standard letters with lists of names and addresses (e.g. libraries, organisations, local firms, etc.).

Internet
If you decide to obtain an Internet account you will be able to tap into a vast source of information. This may be invaluable for researching your book material and may also be useful for identifying likely customers, etc.

- e-mail: you will be able to correspond with customers, colleagues and organisations potentially anywhere in the world.
- Your own Web Site: if you create your own web site you will be able to advertise your work and take orders from an international market. You will be able to publish information about yourself, your product and conduct correspondence with potential buyers.

Fax Facilities
If you do not possess a separate fax machine, you can use your PC to send and receive faxes using software that usually comes free with a modem; the facility to send and receive faxes is a necessity for the small business.

Dictation and Voice Control
Voice activated software is becoming increasingly sophisticated and, although not perfect, it is possible to actually dictate into your PC. The deciphered text can then be tidied up and moved into your DTP document. You will need a sound card in your PC into which a microphone is plugged. Initially, you are required to speak a number of set words into the microphone so that the software can 'learn' your speech mannerisms. Besides being able to dictate, the software will allow you to perform a range of tasks by voice activation. These include opening and closing files, running programs, etc. This facility may be very useful for those who can make only limited use of the keyboard - or for those who prefer dictating rather than typing.

3. Planning The Contents of Your Book

You will undoubtedly have a good idea of the material content of your book. This is the greater part of the battle, having the inspiration and ideas for your intellectual contribution to posterity but.... presentation is also of great importance. Most people who buy books, or for that matter, any other products, are not just looking at the material content. They are also susceptible to texture, packaging and visual impact. Good presentation includes structure, organisation and style; you want people to buy and to enjoy reading your work. If the presentation and layout are good, then it will be easier to read and more pleasing to the reader. Poor presentation, however, is particularly noticeable because it impedes the reader and will soon become irksome. It would be a shame for a book rich in content to be spoilt by poor presentation; effort will be wasted and potential readership lost. The issues we consider in this chapter are format, organisation and style.

3.1 Format, Layout & Style

Format, as described here, is the actual physical form of a book: its size, shape and construction. Modern books can be produced in virtually any size and shape. However, for the small start-up publisher, perhaps using a laser printer and/or the photocopy process, size may be limited by the A4 output format (210m by 297mm). A3 (twice A4) printers, for bigger formats, are available but they are much more expensive so we shall, for the moment, presume that A4 is the basic format. A4 is a good size for certain kinds of book such as guides and technical manuals. A4 can also be trimmed down to a smaller size - but too much will be wasteful on paper. A5 size (148mm by 210mm), which is half that of A4 is an option. If your DTP and/or printer is able to print two adjacent A5 pages per sheet of A4, then this format can be ideal (*see booklet printing*). This book uses the A5 format.

Layout is the manner in which the contents of the book are presented: the page structure, margin size, positions of titles, headings etc. *Style* defines the appearance of the headings and text, the font types, size and weight of the headings and text. You should aim for a style that is simple, unobtrusive and with which you feel 'comfortable'. Remember, you could be working with your chosen style for a considerable length of time. An elaborate one may be awkward to create and maintain and will become tiresome to use after a short time. For ideas on suitable styles, take a closer look at the books on your own shelves, in the library and in book shops. There is no point in 're-inventing the wheel' unless you really have to, so choose one that is pleasing to you and invites the reader to scan through the book. To bear out our comments about poor presentation, see if you can find examples of styles that you do not like and try to identify why. Avoid their displeasing features when you organise your own book.

Simplicity is of the essence, both for the reader and the writer. Do not choose a style that is too fussy, or one that appears cluttered or uses a multitude of fonts. Consider clear chapter headings, sub-headings, a good text font, size and spacing. You will probably find that your DTP package can help you here. For example, Word for Windows holds a number of set styles, which, when selected, will automatically format your document. These can be altered to suit.

You may decide not to finalise styles until your document is almost completed. This is perfectly alright as they can be adjusted during any stage of preparation. If, however, you intend to organise your document into sections and sub-sections, we recommend that you decide their number and scope early on to plan for an even coverage of subject matter throughout the book.

Tailoring Style to your Market

Have regard for your intended audience. You probably would not choose to use the same style for a children's book as one for senior business managers. For example, if you are aiming at readers of an older age group you would, perhaps, choose a slightly larger text size. If you are writing a training manual, consider using wider margins to provide more space for hand-written notes.

3.1.1 Organising by indented levels

For 'information' books, the use of indented headings and text sections can be a very effective way of organising the layout of your book. In a later section, we describe how to create a 'story-board' and show that it is a very effective way of applying precedence and hierarchy to the information you have to impart. Obviously, for other types of book (e.g. non-fiction, poetry etc.) this may be an inappropriate means of organisation but, for putting means, materials and methods across, as in this book, it is ideal. The following is an example showing the use of indentation:

Header Level 1 (e.g. Chapters)

At this level, the text will introduce any concepts and scope of the material that is to be discussed in this section. The text body is indented from the left hand margin of the emboldened heading to give it emphasis.

Header Level 2 (Major sections)

This heading is again emboldened but in a smaller font size. The text is further indented to show its subordinate place in the organisational hierarchy.

Header Level 3 *(Subsection)*
The indentation process has been taken to a further level and again demonstrates the place of the text in the document's hierarchy.

Header Level 3 *(Subsection)*
Subject matter in the same level of hierarchy are indented to the same level.

Header Level 2

And so on, and so on. The overall effect is to give the reader the impression that your book is well organised and has been presented in a logical manner.

This book uses three levels of indentation which we have judged appropriate for the type of material we wish to present. If we had indented to any further level, we would have had trouble in getting an even spread of information throughout all of the sections. Also, the line space left at the lowest level would be very limited - given the extent of the indent distance used. Your DTP will allow you to use as many levels of indent as you can imagine - but common sense should prevail.

This book has been organised thus :

Chapter Headings
18pt, Bold , Underlined
Arial font

1   This is a Level 1 Heading (Chapter)

1cm gap

Text at 10pt underneath this level indented 0.5cm from the heading

12pt, bold, Arial

1.1 This is a Level 2 Heading

Text to go with the level 2 Heading is slightly indented and is printed in 10pt, Times New Roman font.

12pt, bold, Arial, Italic

1.1.1 This is a Level 3 Heading

Text to go with the level 3 Heading. This is also printed in Times New Roman font at 10pt and is indented by 1cm from the margin.

1.1.1 This is Another Level 3 Heading

Text to go with the level 3 Heading.

1.2 This is Another Level 2 Heading

Text to go with the level 2 Heading.

You may have noticed that we have used some indentation in this book and have numbered down to three levels. However, we have only indented the text by 0.5cm at level 2 and by 1cm at level 3. The narrower the columns the fewer words per page and the more paper required. This is wasteful if you are working on narrow margins of profit since the unnecessary consumption of a few extra pages of paper per book soon adds significantly to your material costs. Despite having only a small indentation for each section level, we hope that the overall effect still provides a sufficiently structured look to the book (and without wasting too much paper!)

3.1.2 Section numbering

Numbering is not essential and some readers find it unnecessary. However, in the past we have found that for reference books, people use the Table of Contents to navigate around the book rather than just using the Index. Numbering the section headings does make this easier. Another reason for restricting to three levels is that a section number like 3.1.1 is just about acceptable, whereas 3.1.1.1 and beyond is rather extreme! Three levels looks well balanced in the Table Of Contents (TOC).

> If you intend using section numbering, set your DTP to generate the numbers automatically. Do not number the sections manually as when sections are added or deleted, the heading numbers are automatically re-adjusted.

3.1.3 Amount of text on a page

It is worth remembering that the amount of text you can get on each page is also determined by style, formatting and font sizes. This may not be significant in a short publication (say <50 pages), but the larger the document, the more paper will be used. Too much white space means wasted paper and your book will be less environmentally friendly - and more expensive to produce.

3.1.4 Fonts and font sizes

One of the pleasures of DTP is experimenting with all the fonts at your disposal. With a click of the mouse on the font menu, you can indulge your typographic fantasies! **But be sensible, too many fonts gives a very fussy, cluttered appearance and** if you intend to produce copies of your book using a photocopy process, avoid unnecessarily small text as it will not reproduce well. Similarly, avoid some of the more esoteric fonts which use very narrow line components.

'Fonts', or 'typefaces' are measured in 'point' or pt sizes. For the main body of your document use a 10-12pt size and we also recommend using a fairly conservative font such as Helvetica or NewTimes Roman (as used in this book). These 'serif' fonts are easy to read even at small font sizes (8-10pt) without irritating the reader. Save the more unusual fonts for adding emphasis to such features as headings and examples. Note that this book is written largely using 10pt. To create some contrast with the main body of the text we have used the emboldened Arial font for headings. This is a 'sans-serif' font which, although it looks good at larger point sizes, is not quite so readable at smaller font sizes. Below are some examples of Fonts and Point (pt) sizes for illustration.

Arial 6pt	Times New RomanPS 6pt
Arial 8pt	Times New RomanPS 8pt
Arial 10pt	Times New RomanPS 10pt
Arial 12pt	Times New RomanPS 12pt
Arial 14pt	Times New RomanPS14pt
Arial 16pt	Times New RomanPS 16pt
Arial 18pt	Tms New RmnPS 18pt
Arial 22pt	TmsNewRmnPS 22
Arial 28	TmsNewRmn 28
ArialMT 20	Book Antiqua 22pt
Roman 22	Rockwell 22pt

and…..

Amphion, *Helvetica*, Courier, **Brittanic Bold,** Modern, Roman*Script*, Playbill, **Braggadocia,** *Chancery,* Vagabond, Avian, Optane, **Bordeaux Black,** Boston, *Brush Script,* Futurist, Ghoully Caps, **Hammer Fat,** *Kofee,* Letter Gothic, **Marquee,** Sans Serif, NEON CAPS, Old English, Protege, **STENCIL,** Soutane, …….etc, etc.

3.1.5 Font classification

One of the major divisions between font types is serif and non-serif type faces:

Serif   Non-Serif

(Times New Roman)   (Arial)

Note the little embellishments on the serif font which has hitherto been the most commonly used type in printing. It is believed that these features originated with stone masons finishing off letters with a chisel perpendicular to the rest of the character form. The little hooks and ticks tend to make the characters more distinct and hence easier to read than non-serif fonts. This book uses the Times New Roman font which is quite a conservative one to use. But just for a change, this paragraph uses the Arial font - do you notice a difference in readability?

3.1.6 Special characters and maths notation

The leading DTP packages also include a large number of special characters. There are also typesets for producing mathematical formulae:

Artwork© Brand® Product™

✄ ✓ ✢ ☆ ♥ ➊ ➡ ⇢ ➥ ♣ ♦ ♥ ♠

$$E(S_1) = S - \left(\frac{Ic}{I}\right) - 1\sum_{j=1}^{S}\left(\frac{Ic\text{-}Ij}{I}\right)$$

If your publication requires extensive use of special characters, it is worth checking that the package of your choice provides the ones you require before you start constructing your document (although you could import script from another package).

4. Writing Your Book

We are not providing tuition in creative writing. The material content of your publication is entirely up to you. However, in the light of experience, we give the following advice for organising your manuscript:

4.1 Create a 'Story-board'

This is a device often used in the film industry. The author creates a 'thumbnail' sketch or skeleton of the book using headings and sub-headings, indents etc. This is an excellent method for planning the organisation and coverage of your work. For example, suppose we were about to write this book, how would we organise the contents?

Table of Contents

Preface

> Purpose of the book, audience, anecdote etc.

Chapter 1 Introduction

> Home publishing becoming more popular etc.
> Advantages & disadvantages of established publishers.
> Advantages & disadvantages of home publishing - Low Cost
> etc.

Chapter 2 What you Need

> Hardware
> > Your PC
> > > Specification of components
> > > > Base Unit
> > > > Monitor
> > > > Keyboard
> > > > Mouse
> > Printer
> > > Inkjets and Bubblejets.
> > > Lasers & Ink/Bubble jet.

Advantages & disadvantages.
Scanner
Types
Modems
What are they, what types there are.
Issues
Software
Word Processors
Features to look for etc.

Chapter 3 Planning and Writing Your Book

Style
Format
Storyboard, etc.. etc...

Chapters 4-10......

Any Appendices & Index

There are good reasons for using the story-board approach. Firstly, it sets the scope of the book, the vital elements to be covered and the order in which they will be presented. Secondly, it helps to ensure that all the topics you wish to cover are included and given their correct place and precedence.

Plan the contents of the book in skeleton style and try to achieve even coverage for each topic, this will give balance to your book. It is easier to do this at the outset, with only a few words, than later when you may be dealing with a large and more unwieldy document. If a certain chapter is too long, break it up - with impunity - it costs nothing at the planning stage! The greater the size of the document, the more difficult it becomes to rearrange.

> **Tip:** Avoid extra and tedious work by planning and organising the content at the start of the project.

By the time you have finished this exercise, you will virtually have your Table of Contents (if one is called for), with notes for each section and sub-section, compiled. Writing your book now becomes a matter of filling in the detail below the headings. Of course the layout is not immutable and changes can be made freely but the composition process is made easier when performed within a well organised framework.

4.2 Obeying the Rules of English Grammar

No doubt readers will find faults in the grammar used in this book ...but we have tried to keep to the basic rules. We are particularly indebted to some thought provoking advice sent to us by a reader of our previous book.

Some Rules for Good Writing

📖 Remember to never split an infinitive.

📖 The passive voice should never be used.

📖 Do not put statements in the negative form.

📖 Verbs have to agree with its subjects.

📖 Make sure every word is corectly spelld.

📖 Proof-read carefully to see if you have words out.

📖 If you re-read your work, you can usually find a great deal of repetition can be avoided by re-reading and editing.

📖 A writer must not shift your point of view.

📖 And don't start a sentence with a conjunction.

📖 (Remember too, a preposition is not a good thing to end a sentence with).

📖 Don't! overuse exclamation marks!!!

📖 Place pronouns as close as possible, especially in long sentences, such as those containing ten words or more, to their antecedents.

📖 Writing carefully, dangling participles must be avoided.

📖 If any word is improper at the end of a sentence, a linking verb is.

📖 Take the bull by the hand and avoid mixing metaphors.

📖 Everyone should be careful to use a singular pronoun with singular nouns in their writing.

📖 Always pick on the correct idiom.

📖 And as I've told you a million times: don't exaggerate.

📖 Last but not least, avoid clichés like the plague: seek viable alternatives.

In recent years, there has been a trend towards the use of 'Business' English but to a large extent, this appears to be an excuse for letting standards of grammar slip and good syntax, semantics and punctuation have become casualties in the pursuit of a more abbreviated style. Our own experience in the business world, however, has taught us that accuracy and clarity in communication is of paramount importance. For example, in the area of computer systems design, ambiguities in an analysis document can lead to misinterpretation in a design specification. This in turn leads to errors in the delivered product. Much of this sorry and expensive scenario can be avoided by more careful use of the written word.

All publishing houses demand strict standards in the use of the written word and your fledgling publishing venture should try be no exception. If you are not confident with your use of grammar, employ somebody who is competent and experienced in this area to check your work and help you out. Good writing skills are learnt and improved with practice. It may be worthwhile buying or borrowing books on the subjects of good grammar and writing - there are plenty from which to choose. For the very keen, it may even be worth attending evening classes or weekend workshops on relevant topics.

4.3 Publishing and the Law (as applied in the UK)

There are areas of the law that apply specifically to publishing and of which the author/ publisher ought to be aware. Common sense should prevail but there are a few points to watch. In recent years, high profile court cases, particularly in respect of libel, have proved very costly to authors and publishers found guilty. It would be wise to seek professional advice prior to publication if you believe that you might be transgressing in any of the following areas:

Obscenity
This means, "Tending to deprave or corrupt". In recent years, prosecutions for obscenity have only really applied to pornography, although there have been some infamous cases involving the written word in the past, e.g. D.H. Lawrence's *Lady Chatterley's Lover*.

Libel
Courts are apt to award punitive damages against authors and publishers found guilty of defamation of character. Do not make unsupportable and defamatory statements or false accusations which damage an individual's reputation.

Blasphemy and racial hatred
In the UK, only the Christian faith is covered by the laws of blasphemy and, although not tested in recent years, it is still a criminal offence to blaspheme. However, with Salman Rushdie's 'Satanic Verses' in mind, it would be as well to tread carefully with the major non-Christian faiths. Furthermore, what may not be prosecutable as blasphemy may, through insulting language, be

construed as incitement to racial hatred, which *is* a serious criminal offence in the UK.

Breach of copyright

Plagiarism may be considered the highest form of compliment but it must be avoided. You would not like others to profit from copying your work without authorisation so neither should you incorporate other people's work into your own without written permission. If you want to reproduce extracts of somebody else's copyrighted material, approach the publisher first for their consent but remember that it is usually the author who owns the copyright. If you are able to use such material it is also wise and polite to acknowledge its source. You may be charged for this privilege especially if it is a photograph which may be handled through a photographic agency. Note, that whereas copying exact text is covered by copyright, copying of ideas is not. If you want to use an idea, hypothesis, storyline or whatever, do write it in your own words.

Official secrets and confidentiality

Confidentiality is a very grey area and breaches of it are difficult to prove unless covered specifically by a contract. Many contracts of employment contain clauses about non-disclosure of commercially sensitive information during and even after employment has ceased. The British Official Secrets Act (1911), which is signed by Civil Servants and other crown employees, theoretically provides a virtual blanket ban on disclosure of every piece of information that an employee may obtain during (and after) employment in service to the Crown.

Contempt of court

This relates to a publisher's possible interference with the due course of justice, e.g. by influencing or prejudicing the jury. It is most commonly invoked against newspapers and magazines that pass comment upon the defendants, witnesses and jury members involved in a current court case.

Racial hatred

Words that may be considered to be an "incitement to racial hatred" may result in a prosecution against a publisher.

The above list applies specifically to the UK. If you intend to publish in other countries or export your publications, you may need to seek advice as to whether your work infringes any national laws. Be warned, other countries take a less lenient view in certain areas!

4.3.1 *Reproducing other's copyrighted material*

Most authors are flattered to have their material reproduced in other publications. A short and exact quotation from a paragraph will not usually require prior permission for use - providing you acknowledge the title of the book, author and publisher. For a more substantial reproduction, it is wise to seek permission to avoid any trouble and possible legal expenses later. Songs, music scores, poems, extracts from newspapers and photographs definitely do require permission from the copyright holder ...and be prepared to have to negotiate and pay a fee for the privilege.

Although the copyright is normally owned by the author, it is best to write directly to the publishers. To avoid protracted correspondence the following points should be included in the request:

- The title of the book, publication date and the author for the work you wish to quote.
- The section/ page(s) location of the material you wish to quote.
- A copy of the actual material you wish to quote.
- The title and brief description of your book and when it is to be published.
- A request as to how the author wishes to be acknowledged.

Note that your requests for permission to reproduce material may take some months to be processed and agreed. Make your requests as early as possible - do not wait until just a few weeks before your planned publication date.

4.4 Practical Advice for Maintaining DTP documents

4.4.1 *Organising your PC file directories*

It is advisable to organise your disk files by type and keep them in separate directories (folders if you are using an Apple or the Windows 95 operating system). Your DTP package should be capable of being set to default to specific directories for different file types (images, documents, backups, styles, etc.). It is surprising how fast your files will grow in number - especially successive versions of the same, evolving document. Decide in advance a sensible directory structure for your work, this will help to avoid confusion and mistakes being made. For example:

C:\bookver1\   First version document files
C:\bookver2\....   Subsequent versions
C:\scraps   Scraps of useful text and information
C:\images   Where you keep any scanned pictures etc.
C:\backup   Where you keep back-up copies.
C:\bookdata   Data, spreadsheets, etc.

4.4.2 Standardise headings, text sizes, etc.

Choose suitable styles (fonts and formats) for the various components in your book such as chapter headings, sections, sub-sections and body text. Standardise on them, and avoid 'pick & mix' styles as it becomes more difficult to sort them out later. You need not worry, however, about the minute details (e.g. indentation, spacing above and below section headers). These can be sorted out by applying global changes, i.e. they apply to the whole document, not just to the current sentence, paragraph or page, when all the writing has been finished. If you require heading numbering, use the automatic numbering facilities that your package provides rather than numbering them manually. This option will allow you to add, delete and move sections and retain the correct numbering sequences - important when you come to generate a Table of Contents (TOC) and the Index.

4.4.3 Saving and "backing-up" your work

If you have not experienced accidentally losing current work, then take note. It is extremely frustrating to lose an hour's, morning's or day's worth of creative effort through not saving and backing up your work regularly. By 'backing up' we mean duplicating important files - usually on to floppy disks or magnetic tape cartridges. If you save your files every 10 minutes, then you will not lose more than 10 minutes of your work! It always seems much harder to re-do the work you have already done once. You can use your DTP to save work for you by setting its auto-save facility to run every pre-set number of minutes.

Do not be complacent. Hardware and software faults can happen. Power cuts do occur and equipment can be damaged or stolen ....and of course human error must be taken into consideration - no one is infallible. Be ultra-cautious, save your work on to floppy disks and/or magnetic tape at the end of each day. Your time, which will have been wasted if you have no safe copies of your work, is probably a lot more valuable than the computer equipment - so avoid losing work by being diligent and taking file copies.

> Decide on a file saving / backing-up regime and try to stick to it. Keep your back-up disks or tapes and master software disks safely away from your PC, preferably in another room or building. In the event of catastrophe (fire, theft etc.) you may need to replace your hardware but should have confidence in being able to restore your software packages and a recent version of your working files.

4.4.4 Breaking the document into manageable chunks

As your document gets larger, several things start to happen:

- 📖 It takes longer to save and uses progressively more disk space.
- 📖 It takes longer to move about within it, especially if there are bitmaps of scanned images.
- 📖 It takes longer to load.
- 📖 If you are working intensively on even just one section, and are making regular copies of versions - the *whole* document is saved each time - thereby using a lot of extra disk space.

Software packages (and/or your PC) can become more prone to failure as memory and processor resources become stretched, and their limits of ability to cope are tested. Your PC's operating system employs sophisticated memory management which, when memory is full, transfers parts of its contents to a special disk file ('swap' file). Thus, although the size of your document may exceed the size of computer memory, parts of it, not currently being actively worked on, are written to the swap file. Large documents, with memory hungry objects such as images, tend to cause much memory-to-disk and disk-to-memory transfers (swapping) and this can place a heavy load on disk controllers - which can occasionally get very confused! If there is much swapping, you are also wasting time while you wait for the few seconds necessary for the transfers to take place.

Apart from buying more memory for your PC, the easiest way of alleviating these problems is to break the document into smaller, more manageable chunks, e.g. at the level of chapter. When the document is near completion, the chapters can be joined together again as a single file for polishing. Note also that most packages will let you keep components permanently in separate files but allow you to string them together logically by defining the components within a 'master' document.

> **Tip**: Memory Management: Your PC will try and load as much of your document into its memory as it can. If you do not have enough memory for the whole of a document, the system will start using 'virtual' memory (the swap file). In order to avoid memory faults, you may find it necessary to increase the maximum size to which the swap file is allowed to grow. This file may only be temporary and will release the space used when the PC is turned off. (See the Windows manual for details). If your DTP application and document require a large temporary swap file, ensure that there is sufficient free space on the particular disk drive to allow adequate growth of the swap file (say up to 20Mb). If the file is unable to grow because of lack of space, the application may grind to a halt with a fault!

4.4.5 Images and diagrams

Imported images, e.g. 'bitmaps' of photographs or other objects obtained using a scanner, use a lot of memory and disk file space. Storing and manipulating these images will test the capacity of your system if they are numerous or of large size. If your PC does not have a high processor and memory specification, try to keep their use to a minimum. For illustrations, make use of the drawing facilities in your DTP package to achieve the same or a better result. It is advantageous to use drawing tools in preference to scanned images as you will find that drawings from these tools are much easier to edit. They also take up much less disk space and are far less demanding on your PC's processor.

Here is a nonsense diagram constructed using the drawing facilities in Microsoft Word™ to demonstrate the kinds of diagram that can be created:

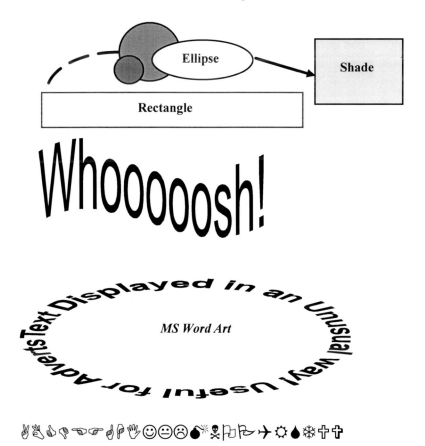

4.4.6 Specialist drawing packages

Besides the drawing capabilities of the DTP package itself, other types of pictures can be created using more specialised packages; very often the package will be a component in an integrated suite of programs. Lotus Ami Pro has a stable mate called Freelance, Microsoft Office has a presentation tool called PowerPoint to go with Word. There are other 'stand alone' packages which can be used to create drawings to be incorporated (imported) into your document, for example, Corel Draw and Harvard Graphics.

4.4.7 ClipArt

Clipart images are generally small pictures or 'clips' and there are many thousands of them available for an author to use. They vary from light-hearted and stylised graphics of everyday objects to photographs of well-known sites, personalities and so on. They can be used to enhance a document as the occasional and well-placed image can
break up the tedium of solid text. Clipart is available in collections of images or 'libraries' usually organised by topic. These are available from a number of sources - your DTP package will probably include one covering a range of subjects. You will find other libraries advertised in computer and specialist magazines offered by software and graphic art companies. The following images are typical examples of those that are provided as standard with DTP packages.

4.4.8 Formatting while working on a document

Whilst working on your document, it is tempting to try and maintain a polished view of your work as it will look for publication. Obviously, arranging pages to best effect (spacing, diagram placement, etc.) is critical to the final product, but while composing and working on the document, you will be inserting and deleting text and images. This will continually affect pagination and will inevitably frustrate your efforts at controlling page breaks in appropriate places (e.g. by adding blank lines before major headings so that they do not appear at the bottom of a page with no following text). This can be particularly noticeable where images are embedded in the text. Images are usually 'anchored' to the appropriate paragraph of text and an image plus its text paragraph occupies a certain amount of space on a page. If extra text from one page is pushed on to the next page that happens to have a diagram, there may no longer be enough physical space for the image plus its anchored text. It will be forced to jump to a fresh page where there is enough space and this ruins any organisation previously intended for the page. This can, to some extent, be countered by putting in 'firebreaks' at appropriate places by inserting 'new page' marks which force a new page to start (these are formatting commands which must be obeyed). Any formatting beyond a new page marker will be insulated from change ...but at some point any unsightly gaps before these page breaks will need to be eliminated by prudent editing.

> **TIP:** Whilst working on the composition of your manuscript, concentrate on the CONTENT. Do not worry too much about the aesthetics of the layout as these can be sorted out afterwards. Trying to maintain the polished view during writing wastes valuable time.

4.4.9 Collaborative writing

The authors of this book have had some experience in collaborative writing ventures. As we work at different locations, we decided that electronic data transfer using modems was the only practicable solution to exchanging documents, text, and images. Although we had identical equipment and software, we still ran into problems, particularly with document formatting. We also initially had a problem with 'version control'. Here is some practical advice on two (or more authors) working on the same book:

Equipment and software
Ensure that all settings, hardware and software are identical, page formats in particular. We found that we had very slight differences in page format. On editing long documents, automatic page formatting ruined the pagination for alternate editors!

Modem settings and communications software
Small files can be exchanged using e-mail over the Internet. For large files, however, we used a product called Laplink (version 5), which allowed us to transmit data between two PCs over the telephone network. We used identical 14,400bps modems and although we thought this task would be trivial it took some time to find the optimum settings and master the technique.

Version control
Agree the overall structure using the storyboard approach, as defined earlier, then break your document into a series of smaller files, e.g. at the chapter level. Each author then becomes the 'owner' of particular chapters at any one time. The

non-owner can only read and make comments upon his/her copy when a new version and/or ownership is transferred from the previous owner. In this way you avoid confusion and both authors can work on (different) parts of the book simultaneously. Be strict about the ownership rules. When nearing completion, the individual elements can be joined together to form a single document - but remember only one author should have ownership of any one section at any one time! Note that if the assembled document is reformatted, changes will be made globally and any individual component settings will be overridden.

5.   Finalising The Manuscript

5.1 Tidying up

When you are happy with the material content of your manuscript, it is time to polish up on the presentation in preparation for the final product. This process requires close attention to detail and a number of rigorous checks. If you are like us, you will begin to think that the book will never be finished! Every time you re-read a section, some alternative phrase, description or viewpoint comes to mind and there is a constant temptation to tinker: adjusting phrases, adding and re-evaluating paragraphs. This is only natural as it is very difficult to be completely objective about one's own work. There comes a time when you must say enough is enough. Determining when you have reached this point is not easy, but we would say that it is when you are no longer adding any new material but merely agonising over phrasing. You will always be able to make small adjustments but leave them for now until after corrections and comments from your proof-reader and or reviewer(s).

5.1.1 Formatting adjustments

There are three main areas for finalising:

1. The material content - under your control as the author/ editor but subject to comments from reviewers.
2. Final presentation - format, layout and style - under your control as editor and typesetter.
3. Preparation of remaining components - Preface, TOC, Index, etc.

Before immersing yourself in the second process, re-apply the spell-checker (and grammar checker if your DTP has one) and give your manuscript a thorough read through, making any obvious corrections to punctuation and syntax. Correct any serious errors now, as the further you go into the final formatting and typesetting, the more disruptive it becomes when significant amounts of material are added or deleted. Insertions and deletions can cause a surprising level of disturbance to the overall format as pagination is adjusted automatically.

Print out a copy of the working manuscript and if you have a collaborator, spouse, friend or anyone who is reasonably literate and willing to read it, ask them to scrutinise it. It is surprising how an individual's mind works along 'tram lines'; you do not notice quite glaring errors which are maddeningly obvious to others because you are focusing on other issues. These errors are miraculously detected by a fresh mind - which has a different set of tram lines! A more thorough proof-read should be performed later but an early scrutiny by another reader will iron-out the most obvious flaws and errors.

When you are happy that the material content is satisfactory, you can start polishing up your manuscript for publication. The following items will help this process:

General layout and style. Do these first as they affect your document 'globally' by influencing the amount of text that can be printed on a page. Warning - if you make adjustments later, your careful arrangements of text and diagrams will be rearranged by automatic adjustments to pagination.

- Make any final adjustments to page set-up options, e.g. format (A4, A5, page margins).
- Finalise heading styles (font, size, bold/ italic, spacing between lines, section numbering, indentation, etc.).
- Finalise paragraph styles (fonts, size, etc.).
- Headers and footer style.
- Optional: adjust sections at chapter level so they always start on the same facing page (usually on odd pages only).

Specific adjustments to text. These are more local adjustments that improve the text appearance but do not significantly alter text layouts on subsequent pages.

- Replace double spaces after punctuation marks with single spaces thereby avoiding 'rivers of text'.
- Where the DTP justification has spread words out across a line, consider adjusting the text to give a more even appearance.
- Check for consistency of line spacing, for example after headings, between paragraphs, diagrams.
- Check consistency of bullet-point indentations.
- Adjust spacing/ content of pages so that a page throw does not fall at an inappropriate point in a paragraph, list or diagram. Aim to give pages a well balanced and pleasing appearance.
- Check for any other inconsistencies in text layout (any remaining should be picked up by your proof-readers).

5.1.2 *Page set-up: margins and printable area*

The area that your printer is physically able to print within does not always correspond with what you see on the monitor. Care must be taken to ensure that the margin settings for your document are inside the printer's accessible printing area. This is only a problem if your layout approaches the edges of the paper and is best determined by trial and error. Even for a standard setting of, say, A4, the printable areas can vary slightly between different printers. You may perhaps have noticed that in most books, the left and right page margins are of different widths. This can be for aesthetic reasons, but also because an extra width may be needed for the binding. Depending on the binding process, you may need to leave an extra wide margin (called the gutter) so that the edge of the text is a sufficient distance away from the fold. To determine how wide the margins should be on each side, you will need to know how much margin will be consumed by the binding in the middle and how much will be trimmed off on the outside edge (if any).

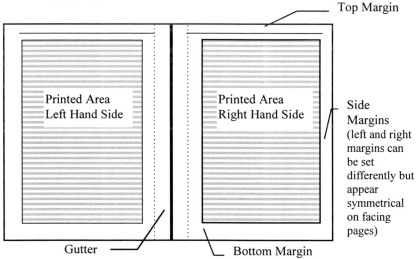

Different width left and right margins can be achieved in two ways:

1) Ensure that the printed area is dead centre on the page. The offset effect is then created by appropriate guillotining during the binding process. This is the easiest solution. Note, however, that just because the page appears centred on the PC monitor, it does not necessarily mean that it is centred on the printer output. Trial and error are required to find the correct margins for your particular printer.

2) You can use 'page set-up' in your DTP package to set different margin settings for facing pages. This is easy where you can print multiple pages per sheet of paper (see Booklet printing) but beware, for single pages this can be

difficult to get right. You need to experiment by printing on both sides of your paper; this task is simplified if you have a duplex printer as it automatically prints on both sides of the paper. If you do not have a duplex printer, then the following method can be used:

- 📖 Set up your page margins for facing pages.
- 📖 Print *odd* numbered pages for a portion of your book.
- 📖 Put the printed pages back into the printer paper feeder, the reverse side up, to print on opposite sides.
- 📖 Print the *even* numbered pages for the same page range.

Hopefully, the margins will now be set to the same distance from the edge, on both sides of the paper. Most DTPs will allow you to print odd and even pages selectively and if your printer does not have duplex options you should be able to put the same batch of paper in twice (i.e. to print on the reverse side). Do be very careful not to bend or damage the output - you certainly do not want any paper jams while printing the reverse sides.

5.1.3 Headers & footers

If appropriate for your particular work, the appearance of your document may be enhanced using 'headers and footers'. They may just be narrow lines at the top and bottom of the page, but they can also carry some heading text that can vary from page to page to highlight the contents of a particular page. So that they do not become too obtrusive, it is usual to make their font sizes slightly smaller than the normal text. Once set up, headers and footers will automatically run through your document occupying an area outside the main page area. The depth and width of headers and footers can be adjusted to suit.

For example, a header placed at the top of the page could take the form:

Page 22

Chapter title or Running Header

Page Text..........

Similarly a footer, which appears below the main text area may look as follows:

Home Publishing   ©1997

(The copyright mark may help to deter unauthorised photocopying by identifying the publication on every page!)

5.1.4 Position of new chapter pages

It is common practice to start page numbering and new chapters on a right-hand facing page. (In the interests of paper conservation, however, you may decide against this as you may waste a few extra pages if blanks need to be inserted to achieve this.) If you wish to follow this convention, insert any appropriate 'new page' markers at the end of chapters to ensure that the next chapter starts on the correct facing page. Assuming page 1 starts on a right hand page, all subsequent chapters will always start on an odd numbered page. Your DTP may be able to automate this for you.

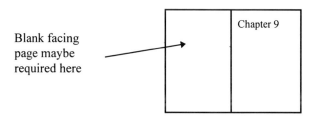

This may result in a complete blank page being inserted before a new chapter if the text for the previous chapter does not finish on a left-hand page.

5.1.5 Formatting paragraph text

The appearance of paragraph text is an extensive subject in its own right and we would recommend buying or borrowing a DTP book that covers this topic in more detail. There are a number of specific points concerning the actual appearance of the text and fonts which will separate the professional from the beginner. At first glance, many of these points go completely unobserved to the casual reader but will nonetheless enhance the appearance of the text. The more obvious ones that the self-publisher should be aware of, are listed below:

1. *Text justification.* This is the alignment of text in relation to a margin. A paragraph can be left-justified, right-justified, centred or fully justified (both left- and right-hand edges of paragraphs are lined up). Most modern publications are fully justified, as this book is. For contrast, however, the preceding paragraph is left-justified - which is fine for poetry but not as appropriate for a book of this type.

2. *Word spacing.* The problem with justifying text is that it can create uneven gaps between words as the DTP program pads the lines out to a fixed length. Do not use double spaces at the end of a sentence because this can cause artificially large gaps to open up between the last word in one sentence and the first word of the next. Different packages handle this situation with varying degrees of effectiveness. Big gaps between words

have a habit of lining themselves up in a displeasing way to create 'rivers of text'. By keeping to single spaces after sentences, these gaps are minimised. If the text alignment results in some ugly spacing, it is possible to improve the appearance by rephrasing the text.

5.2 Conventional Book Structure

The structure of most books follows a standard convention and we detail the components below. Some inclusions are optional, single page, and need not be included in page numbering so remember this when calculating the overall page count.

I. The first page of the book is known as the 'half-title'(or 'bastard title') and consists of the main title only.

II. The reverse side (verso) of page I is usually left blank but some books carry advertising material on it.

III. The Title Page: this contains the main title and a sub-title, if applicable, the author(s) names, the publisher and their address. If there are any other significant contributors, such as editor, illustrator or writer of a foreword, these may also be included here.

IV. On the reverse of III is the Copyright Page.

V. Acknowledgements (optional). If these are extensive it may be better to place them at the back of the book.

VI. A Dedication/ Quotation (optional).

VII. Foreword (optional).

VIII. Preface (optional).

IX. Table of Contents (strongly advised for non-fiction).

X. List of Figures and Illustrations (optional).

XI. *The main text. This may commence with an Introduction. Page numbering normally starts here and continues through to the end of your last chapter.*

XII. Any Glossary of Terms, Bibliography, useful contacts/ addresses, Appendices (page numbered).

XIII. The Index (page numbered).

----------- Page numbering stops here ------------

XIV. Any advertising for other books you may have published (optional).

5.2.1 The Copyright Page

This page, on the verso (reverse side) of the title page, is your declaration of copyright. The precise format varies from book to book but the following elements should be included:

- When it was first published and any subsequent editions.
- The Imprint (the publisher, their address, telephone no., fax etc.)
- The copyright mark with the year and copyright holder of the form: "Copyright © 1997 Peter Domanski"*
- "All rights reserved...." Clauses. These assert your rights as the copyright holder and give notice regarding the unauthorised reproduction of your work.
- British Library CIP notification. Include the phrase "British Library Cataloguing-in-Publication Data. A catalogue record for this book is available from the British Library" (or, e.g. Library of Congress Cataloguing in Publication Data in the USA).
- The ISBN number.
- The typesetter, printers/ binders, the typeset used (optional).
- Any notes regarding liability, good faith, etc.
- Acknowledgements of trademarks.
- Any short notes, assertions or declarations, e.g. "printed on 100% re-cycled paper"

*The symbol © indicates copyright world-wide. This special symbol should be available as part of the symbol repertoire for your DTP. For an example of the copyright page see the one at the beginning of this book.

5.2.2 Acknowledgements

This may take a whole page if there is sufficient material to warrant it. Include collaborators, contributors, suppliers and any people who have helped significantly with the preparation. Among the people acknowledged might be photographers, illustrators, authors of other copyrighted material you may have used. If there are a substantial number of credits, it may be preferable to place this section at the end of the book.

5.2.3 Foreword

A foreword is usually written by someone of fame or eminence. It is used to introduce your work and give it additional kudos or extra credibility and authority. If you feel that a foreword would be of benefit, draw up a shortlist of possible candidates. You might consider your local MP, Bishop, a Company Chief Executive, Aristocrat or renowned expert in your field. Look in Who's Who and other directories for ideas. Remember, they may be equally flattered to be asked, as you are to have your invitation accepted. (Ask only one VIP at a time as simultaneous acceptances could cause you great embarrassment!) Do consider publication timescales and politely suggest a copy deadline as it would be frustrating to wait extra weeks or months for this final material.

5.2.4 Preface

The Preface can be used to introduce your subject and outline your particular philosophy and views. Many authors use it to explain why they wrote the book and may use anecdotes. It can be an invaluable device for summarising your work, so use it well. Potential buyers, browsing in a book shop, will often read the Preface - as will reviewers who may draw on it for any write-ups. Here is the place to display your personality and invite the customer to read on! If you think your subject needs further introduction, say more than a couple of pages, then include an Introduction as a separate section instead of combining it into the Preface.

5.2.5 Table of Contents (TOC)

Your DTP package should be able to generate a Table of Contents (TOC) automatically and in a variety of styles. The TOC comprises the headings and sub-headings used throughout the document along with the corresponding page numbers. Some packages may generate the TOC as a separate document that you can paste in at the beginning of your main document (but watch the page numbering!). Others, including Microsoft Word, will allow you to create a TOC at the beginning of your document and compensate automatically for the extra pages that it will use. You can generate and regenerate a TOC whenever you like but, remember, a TOC will very quickly become out of date and unsynchronised with the page numbering if you generate it whilst still working on the document. This is because headings and their numbers (if used) can be re-sequenced and/or the page numbers altered. We recommend leaving TOC generation until the composition of the document has been completed.
See the Table of Contents pages at the beginning of this book for a typical example.

5.2.6 Glossary, Bibliography, Appendices, etc.

Many reference works refer to a great deal of information that is not always presented in the body of the book itself. Instead, additional and explanatory material is contained in reference sections which are appended at the back of the book, usually before the Index.

Glossary

If you are using a lot of technical terms and acronyms, list them together with short explanations in a glossary. This can be very helpful for those readers new to the subject and who could easily be confused by a plethora of unfamiliar terms and jargon.

Bibliography and References

If you draw on, or refer to material from other published sources, it is usual to acknowledge it. This can be done at the end of each chapter or as a separate section at the back of the book. For technical and scientific works there are standard referencing conventions for abbreviating journal titles. Where other authors' works are cited more than once, it is more convenient to place the references at the back of the book and number them - usually in order of appearance. These numbers can then be used in the text. Your DTP may well have a facility for drawing up a bibliography or reference list.

Contact Addresses

List names and addresses of useful organisations and other contacts. If possible, include the telephone, fax numbers and e-mail addresses as well. *Check that this information is still correct and current before publication.*

Further Reading

List other publications that the reader may find useful to broaden their knowledge on the subject; by listing other works, you are providing a better resource book for your readers than if you failed to include them.

Appendices

An appendix is where accompanying data, tables, detailed information, additional methods, formulae, case studies, etc. should be included. If incorporated in the main body of the book, these would be a distraction and spoil its flow. You can use as many appendices as you want. If your subject is a fast changing one, e.g. computers, science and economics, then consider moving as much of the 'dynamic' information into appendices as you can. When you come to revise your book for a new edition, most changes will be concentrated in the appendices, so minimising the overall revision of your book.

> **Tip:** It is sensible to keep these sections as separate documents in separate files. When the book is nearing completion, they can be inserted into your main document before generating the TOC and index. By keeping these accessory documents small and separate, editing them will be quicker and it will also help reduce the size of your main working document.

5.2.7 Creating an Index

There is a Society of Indexers for professional practitioners of the art - such are the specialist skills required to create a good Index. Modern DTP packages, however, have made generating an index simple, once you get the hang of it! First, though, you will need to read through your document and select the specific words and components in the text that you would like to included in the Index. In our experience, this is best achieved by printing a draft copy and marking with a highlighter pen the words in the text you wish to reference in the index. When this exercise is complete, instruct the DTP which words in the document you wish to use by marking them with Index 'tags'.

Tagging words for Index entry is achieved by placing the mouse cursor on a word and inserting an index tag either from a toolbar option or, alternatively, by entering a short-cut key sequence on the keyboard. Index marks can be set to appear in a different colour from the text, so they stand out whilst viewing the document on the screen; they do not appear in the text when printed. Indexes can contain multi-levels and so you can position an Index item under an appropriate classifying key word, e.g. 'File creation' can be devised as 'creation' underneath the keyword of 'Files'.

Files, 25, 29
      creating, 25, 37, 43
      deleting, 25, 38
      types, 25
Font, 48, 53, 72
etc.....

As you progress through the document making Index marks, the repertoire of Index entries that you can attach to the words in the text becomes more and more extensive. As the Index marks are attached to individual words, it does not matter if the relative positions of the tagged words are moved around the text as the markers follow them.

Like the TOC, the Index can be created within the main document or as a separate document (depending on the DTP package), by selecting a 'generate index' menu option. Your DTP should provide you with a variety of styles to choose from. Our advice is the same for Indexes as for the TOC. Do not generate your Index until you have finished editing the document - otherwise it too becomes out of date as the relative page numbering is changed. **Warning**: Always check carefully that the TOC and Index generation functions have worked correctly. These processes are prone to pick up misplaced headings, page breaks and hidden tags. (For example, in MS Word, Index tags placed in headings will create extra heading lines in the TOC.)

It is worth remembering that the default page format settings and fonts used for the separate Index and TOC documents may not match those of the main document. They should be amended to comply with your standard document style and format settings.

5.3 Print Process: Specific Tips for Photocopying

If you decide to produce your books initially using the photocopy process, you will need to make sure that all the text and pictures are satisfactorily reproduced. As previously mentioned, avoid font sizes of less than 8pt, but also check shading, diagrams and images.

The less featured packages and printers do not produce true grey scale; the varying degrees of grey are achieved by stippling and hatching (shades of grey made of fine cross-hatching). These do not reproduce very well, if at all, when photocopied so avoid their use in diagrams and shaded table headings, etc. Likewise, very fine, whiskery lines on diagrams and scanned images will sometimes not reproduce at all.

> Before committing yourself to a large photocopying run, it is as well to do a few test runs to see that the quality is satisfactory; if necessary, avoid the use of less solid objects. If you must use solid greys, consider applying Letraset™ film shading to your document, which should give a more satisfactory result.

5.4 Proof-reading

After you have applied the spell-checker utility, read and reread your document. When you are happy with it, give it to somebody else to read, someone who you can rely on, for both their English language skills and objectiveness. It would be well worth paying someone such as a teacher, librarian, newspaper proof-reader, etc. for their services. It is imperative that your script is checked for correct sentence construction, punctuation and good grammar. You will probably be surprised by the number of errors they identify - even simple things such as transposed and missing words. You must eliminate these errors before they are found by paying customers!

> **Tip:** For proof-reading your own work, do not always start reading from the beginning of the document, as fatigue seems to set in at about the same place each time! Alter your reading strategy, start reading from the last chapter, then the previous one... and so on. In this way you can apply your concentration more evenly throughout the book.

5.4.1 *Proof reading conventions*

You may decide to employ an experienced proof-reader to ensure that your manuscript reads well and attains a high standard of grammatical correctness. There is a standard set of notations that your proof-reader is likely to apply to your text. The following is just a subset, but probably covers the most commonly used symbols for text correction:

Margin Symbol	Example of use	Meaning
≡	obey the rules peter	Change to upper case
≠	Use Small letters Here	Change to lower case
⌒	Close up the gap	Close the gap
σ	Take out a character	Remove characters
#	Insert spacehere	Insert a space
⋀ text	Insert in here	Insert extra text
⊔⊓	letters are transposed / words transposed are	Transpose characters
∿	Emphasise these words	Embolden
⊔⊣	*Change* from italic	Change to upright
⊔⊔	Change to Italic	Change to italic
⸜	Writers need ideas	Insert apostrophe
⊙	Finish with a period	Insert full stop (period)
⸝/	and inevitably a comma	Insert a comma
:/	Here are some more	Insert a colon
;/	A semi-colon needed	Insert a semi-colon
=/	Domanski Irvine	Insert a hyphon
⸌ ⸍	He shouted Hello	Quotation marks
c/)	Use a new pen	Parenthesis
⊏	Move text left	Move text left
⊐	Move text right	Move text right
	never again. The next day	New paragraph
	never again. / However, no sooner	Run together
─<	A line of text / Another line of text	Insert space between lines
→	A line of text / Another line of text	Less space between lines

> **IMPORTANT**
> *In our experience, the proof-reading/ reviewing/ editing cycle is a critical phase in any publishing project. IT MUST NOT BE SKIMPED. Do not attempt to cut corners even though this can be a very tiresome exercise during the final stages. Care and attention to detail will pay dividends. Do not even think about going to print until you are absolutely sure spelling and grammar are correct. Get as many impartial readers as you can for corrections, suggestions and constructive criticisms; you may need to pay them - at the very least offer them a finished book for their contribution to your project.*

5.4.2 Peer review

Perhaps you are contemplating publishing your own work because you are unable to attract a publisher to do it for you? You may, like many before you, have been rejected because the publisher does not consider the material suitable, because it may not be of sufficient novelty or quality or you might have been defamatory or libellous. If this is the case then you should not let vanity get the better of you and publish regardless. You certainly would not want to publish, find out too late and be sued. As a publisher of your own works, you have the same responsibility for truth and accuracy as any other publishing company - but you will have fewer resources available to you so an extra duty of care is placed upon you.

Get a second and third opinion on your book by a process of 'peer review'. If you have tried to get articles published in journals and other publications, you will know all about this! If your book is non-fiction, we strongly recommend that you find one or two independent parties to review your work for accuracy or validity of content. All publishers have an editorial staff and access to specialists to ensure the integrity of any work that they publish - they have reputations to protect - and so have you!

You may have spent so long writing and formatting your book, and become so emotionally involved with it that you are no longer sufficiently objective to see even the most obvious flaws. The brain tends to think along tram-lines and when you read something with which you are very familiar, you tend to skip words and even phrases. Even obvious errors are overlooked in this way. A fresh, objective mind will do wonders; clearing up ambiguities, querying points made and generally taking a critical view of your work. When the results of this reviewing exercise have been digested and assimilated, you will feel a lot more confident in the validity and worth of your efforts. This is important when the time comes to promote and sell your book.Getting Published.

6. Getting Published

6.1 Choosing a Title and the Importance of Keywords

A good title for your book is imperative. Whereas an 'abstract' or esoteric title is acceptable for a work of fiction, a reference book or other factual type of work will rely largely on the title to attract the attention of book buyers, researchers, librarians, etc. It is a very competitive world and your subject may well be covered by other authors and publishers. It is essential, therefore, that your title reflects as accurately, and as fully as possible, the theme and content of the book. This has become increasingly important because of the growth of electronic search methods to locate book titles by one or more keywords. Faced with a mass of titles on an initial keyword search, a librarian or researcher may apply further keywords as extra selection criteria to narrow down the list to the most appropriate looking titles. Your book could be passed over because the title is not selected by either a broad initial search or a subsequent more specific search. It is, therefore, essential to use an apt and synoptic title.

Short and punchy titles are usually the most effective. Try not to use more than five to six words. If you really want to use an abstract title, you could use a sub-title for further explanation, for example:

Title:"The Old Slow Road"
Sub-title: "Rediscovering the Drovers' Routes of England "

Taking this book as an example, it took us some time to arrive at the title and along the way we rejected the following earlier attempts:

"A Guide to Low Cost Publishing "

"Home Publishing"

"DIY Publishing"

"How to Publish and Market your Own books"

"Desk Top Publishing and Marketing Techniques "

Each of these titles would have been acceptable; however, none of them provides a complete enough description of the book's scope and contents. It is wise to assume that a customer or borrower will be seeking out information on titles by keyword searches. Although a long title, we hope that the keywords in our final choice: *"A Practical Guide to Publishing Books Using Your PC"* creates the following expectations in the mind of the potential reader:

"A Practical Guide "

- Implies that the book is going to advise me on how to achieve something in a straightforward manner - practical application rather than theory.

"Publishing Books "

- I expect advice on the publication process.

"Using Your PC"

- The book will show me how I can use my PC (or, if I haven't got a PC, what I will need).

The sub-title, *"Organising, Writing, Printing & Marketing Your Own Books"* tells me that the book is going to give me advice in these key areas which together appear to offer a comprehensive coverage of the subject.

We hope to have cast a wide net by using appropriate keywords that are subjects in their own right. In its entirety, the title infers that the book is going to cover the whole process - from writing to selling. We were careful not to be too technologically oriented as many people are wary of, or intimidated by, words like "DeskTop Publishing" or "Internet".

If you do want to use a more abstract title, you can still provide some keywords by incorporating a sub-title. For example:

"Out of the Frying Pan: Economical Recipes for Students ".
"Life on the Edge: A Report of Homelessness in the Inner City ".

Without wishing to labour the point, it is very important that for works of non-fiction, the title not only reveals the scope of the book to your audience but also incorporates appropriate keywords. This point will be further reinforced when we discuss the use of the Internet for marketing purposes.

6.2 ISBN

As a publisher, what other criteria should you consider? Of great importance is the ISBN number (International Standard Book Numbering):

e.g. The number for this book is: ISBN 0-9526043-2-9

The ISBN should be prominently displayed on the Copyright page (the reverse of the title page) and, most importantly, on the bottom right-hand side of the back cover.

ISBN numbers are world-wide, unique numbers issued to publishers to allocate to their publications. Nearly every book published has an ISBN number (ISSNs for journals, newsletters, etc.). It gives each publication a unique registered identity.

The first part of an ISBN identifies the country or country grouping. The 0 (or alternatively 1) identifies the English speaking nations (UK, USA, Australia & New Zealand, English-speaking Canada, Zimbabwe, Puerto Rica, South Africa). The second part identifies the publisher: 952 for   Domanski-Irvine Book Co. The third part, 60432 identifies the book title/edition for a publisher. The last digit, 9, is a 'check digit' that is artificially created using an algorithm to check the validity of the ISBN number.

> **ISBN numbers are used by publishers, libraries, distributors and book shops for ordering and stock identification purposes. If you intend to sell any books through these channels, an ISBN number will be essential. Apply for a number(s) in plenty of time. In the UK, you will be registered as a publisher free of charge.**

6.2.1 What kinds of publications do ISBNs cover?

ISBNs are used primarily to number books uniquely; however, they are also applied to:

☐ Pamphlets and booklets.
☐ Loose-leaf publications, e.g. in ring binders.
☐ Mixed media publications, e.g. books with CD ROMS, films and video.
☐ Books on audio cassettes.
☐ PC software.
☐ Electronic media containing printable reading material.
☐ Publications in Braille.
☐ Maps.

6.2.2 What ISBNs do not cover

📖 Ephemeral material such as diaries, calendars, advertisements.
📖 Art material with no text.
📖 Sound recordings.
📖 Serial publications (see ISSN numbers).

6.2.3 Why are ISBNs useful?

If someone orders a book from a bookshop and the ISBN is known or identified, it is a simple matter of looking up the publisher's reference number to get details for ordering. *ISBNs are used by bookshops, distributors, cataloguers. They are used to identify both book title AND publisher.*

It is in your interest to register your book with an ISBN number. This does not give you copyright protection BUT it does mean that details of your book will be passed on to distributors and wholesale book purchasers. ISBN numbers are issued free in the UK by the Standard Book Numbering Agency Ltd. which is part of J. Whitaker and Sons Ltd. Their address is:

J. Whitaker and Sons Ltd.,	Tel. 0171 420 6000
12 Dyott Street,	Fax 0171 836 4342
London WC1A 1DF	e-mail isbn@whitaker.co.uk.

(See the appendix for addresses for some non-UK ISBN Agencies)

Write or telephone to request an application form for an ISBN number(s). This is a service for publishers, not authors, so if you are not known to them already as a publisher they will require you to give some evidence of your intention to publish. (A Title page and publishers' details on the reverse side will be adequate.) You will be allocated a publisher's reference number (which forms a number prefix of the ISBN) and, if requested, they will provide you with a block of pre-allocated ISBN numbers to use for your publications. They will also provide you with a useful information pack concerning ISBN usage and British Library cataloguing.

Upon receipt of your ISBN number(s), complete and return the forms to give details about your forthcoming publication. Whitaker's need at least three month's notice before the intended publication date. This gives them time to add your title to "New Titles" lists for circulation to book buyers, libraries, etc. (A useful form of free advertising in itself!).

6.2.4 Rules for use of ISBN numbers

The agency that allocates the numbers to you (Whitaker's in the UK) can provide you with a booklet describing the rules in respect to allocating numbers. The most important ones are listed below:

- Each edition of a publication must have a separate ISBN number.
- If the book is sold in different bindings (hardback, softback) each version should have a separate ISBN number.
- You need not use a new ISBN number if you change the cover design but you will need a new one if you change the binding (e.g. softback to hardback).

6.3 The CIP and Book Information form

In the UK, the Cataloguing In Publication programme is a scheme run by the British Library. It is a standard reference given to books for easy identification and is of particular use to libraries. It involves key-words and an allocated reference number. A 'CIP block' was once a common feature of the copyright page on the reverse side of the title page and it took the form:

BRITISH LIBRARY CATALOGUING IN PUBLICATION DATA

A Guide to British Sheep Breeds
    1. Great Britain.   Livestock.   Rare Breeds.

    I. Domanski, Peter

    186.123456789

    ISBN 0-952-60432-6

This is an optional not mandatory feature. You are, however, obliged to send a copy of your publication to the British Library for reference purposes. (See later note on legal requirements).

This is a representation of the Whitaker CIP/ Book information form (complete it at least three months before your publication date).

Whitaker/CIP Book Information

Whitaker Biblioaraohic Services. 12 Dvott Street.
London WC1A 1DF . T0171836 8911 F01713795469

Please complete all sections as fully as possible and return with Prelims (title page, title page verso, contents page etc.)

The British Library has advised publishers that a CIP print block is no longer necessary. Simply print the following on the title page verso: **British Library Cataloguing in Publication Data. A catalogue record for this book is available from the Brithish Library.**
NB. CIP is only available for titles notified to us pre-publication
☐ If you feel a CIP block is necessary, please tick, otherwise you will not receive one

Contact name in case of auerv	Date of oublication		
Teleohone number	Dav	Month	Year

1 ISBN	2 Price £	net/non	3 Binding	☐ Cloth	Other (specify)
ISBN	Price £	net/non	(✓)	☐ Paperback	Other (specify)

4 Author(s) and date(s) of birth where known Surname first followed bv other names	Editor(s) or Reviser(s) Surname first

5 Translator(s) Surname first	Lanauaae from which translated

6 Title

Sub-title

7 Height (in cms)	8 No of pages	No of volumes (if sold as a set)	9 No and type of illustrations

10 Edition (✓) First ☐ New☐ Reprint☐ Revised☐ Facsimile ☐	Illustrator(s)
Date of original edition tion	No of edition	Original Publisher

11 Name of series & volume no
ISSN

12 Brief description of subject matter	13 Place of publication

Whitaker general classification

Children's reading key	Religious classification (if applicable)

If the book is Adult Fiction (✓)
☐ General   ☐ Romance   ☐ War
☐ Historical   ☐ Science Fiction   ☐ Western
☐ Mystery (inc Crime)   ☐ Short Stories

14 Readership level
☐ Children   ☐ Tertiary   ☐ General
☐ Primary   ☐ Postgraduate   ☐ Fiction
☐ Secondary   ☐ Prof

15 Imprint on title page

16 Name of publisher (and address if not a PA member)	17 Name and Address of distributor (if not the same as publisher)

Instructions provided by Whitaker's for completing the CIP / Book Information form:

Whitaker / CIP Book Information Forms.

Why use them?

Information supplied to Whitaker on these forms will be distributed to booksellers and librarians in 106 countries. Eligible book information will also be supplied to the British Library's Cataloguing in Publication programme.

The information is published weekly, monthly and annually and will appear in a variety of Whitaker products including *The Bookseller*, Bookbank, Whitaker's microfiche products and bound annual volumes of *Whitaker's Books in Print* and *Whitaker's Book List*. The information is also used by TeleOrdering to route orders from booksellers and librarians to publishers.

Whitaker book information is also supplied to users by online networks including Dialog, Blaise and BLCMP.

To ensure entry into the British Library's CIP programme, book details must be supplied at **least three** months in advance of publication. Provisional details concerning titles may be given, provided any changes are notified to us. Pre-printed postcards are available free on request for this purpose. Alternatively, please contact Whitaker' Bibliographic Services to discuss other proposals for updating.

Filling in the forms

1 ISBN
A separate ISBN is required for each edition. Full information concerning the rules for allocating ISBN's can be obtained from the UK International Standard Book Numbering Agency, 12 Dyott Street, London WC1A 1DF

2 Price
The retail price should be quoted in £ sterling. UK publishers and distributors should indicate whether the book is being sold as a net or non-net item.

3 Bindings
Apart from Cloth (or Cloth type) and Paperback. Other major binding types are Leather, ½ Leather, ¼ Leather, Laminated Boards, Limp Cloth and Spiral. If unbound please indicate whether sold in folder, binder, box etc. If the item is a map please indicate whether it is sold folded or flat.

4 Author(s) and Editor(s)
Please give only those authors and editors who appear on the title page of the book.
The surname should be given first. Forenames or initials must always be given. If more than three authors or editors are responsible for the book only the first three names need be given. The names of "series" editors should not be given. Give date of birth where known.

5 Translator(s)
The surname should be given first. If the name of the translator is not known The language from which the book was translated should still be provided. If the book is not wholly printed in the English language then details of the other languages printed should be noted.

6 Title and Sub-title
The full title and sub-title should always be given as presented on the title page. They should not be abbreviated or truncated in any way. If the book has a volume or part number or, in the case of an annual, a year of issue, then this should be given as a part of the title.

7 Size
Please give the overall height of the book in centimetres. If landscape then the height and width should be given.

8 Pagination
The total number of pages in the book should be given. If prelims are present and, numbered separately, then the number for these pages should be given before that of the number for the main text, eg xv,193.

9 Illustrations
Illustrations, diagrams, figures, tables, charts and maps should be noted. It should also be specified whether they are in black and white or colour.

10 Edition
A "First" edition is a text which is being published for the first time in a particular country.

A "New" edition is the republication of a book where the text has not been altered to any significant degree, but where binding, format, series, imprint or title have changed.

A "Reprint" is the republication of a book where no significant changes have been made to the text and the binding, format, series and imprint also remain the same.

A "Revised" edition is a text which is being republished with significant changes made to it.

Changes to binding, format, series or imprint may also have been made, but these, by themselves, do not entitle a book to be defined as a revised edition.

A "Facsimile" edition is an exact copy of a text usually made by photographic or xerographic reproduction.

11 Series
Only names of series which are present on the title page should be supplied.

12 Classifications
If no descriptive or prelim material is available, please give a brief description of the subject matter of the book. Alternatively please allot a Whitaker classification. If a title is eligible for an inclusion in our specialist publication *Religious Books in Print* then the relevant special classification should also be provided.

The Children's Reading Key should be supplied for *all* relevant titles.

Copies of all classification schedules are available from Whitaker Bibliographic Services, free upon request.

13 Place of Publication
Country of residence of publisher, **not** place of printing.

14 Readership Levels
Explanatory notes are available for those who require further information.

15 Imprint
The publisher's imprint should be supplied as present on the title page.

16 Publisher
Name of Publisher should be supplied, and address if not a member of the Publisher's Association.

17 Distributor
Details only to be supplied if they differ from the publisher's.

Please ensure that Whitaker Bibliographic Services is on your mailing list and receives copies of all promotional material and catalogues.

For further details, or to order supplies of forms, please contact:

Whitaker
Bibliographic Services
12 Dyott Street, London WC1A 1DF
T0171 836 8911   F0171 379 5469.

The British Library advises that it is no longer necessary to have a CIP block included on your copyright page (reverse side of the title page). The following words are all that are required. **"British Library Cataloguing in Publication Data. A catalogue record of this book is available at the British Library"**. If you want one, then a CIP 'block' is obtained by application well before publication (tick the relevant box on the Whitaker/CIP form).

Before publication, you should complete the combined Whitaker/CIP Book Information form which is sent to you when your ISBN number(s) are allocated. Complete the form and return it to Whitaker's (the UK bibliographic services agents) who will include your book information on their New Books lists. Three month's notice is required prior to publication. This information alone can sell books as the lists are distributed to the book trade, major libraries, etc. Once you are properly registered, anyone walking into a shop can order your book using the ISBN number.

> **Do complete the Whitaker/CIP Book Information form** (for publication in the UK). This information will be used in New Books listings which are widely distributed to book buyers. It costs nothing and it can even result in sales without any further work on your behalf!

6.4 Publishing Legalities

6.4.1 Legal requirements (UK): Book Depositions

Publishers in the UK are required by law to deposit a copy of each book they publish at the British Library. As soon as your book is printed, send a copy to the following address:

Legal Deposit Office,
The British Library,
Boston Spa,
Wetherby,
West Yorkshire LS23 7BY

Tel. No. 01937 546612

84

If you do not send one under your own volition, several months later you will receive an official request from the Legal Deposit Office. As publisher, you are also required to provide copies to the following institutions, free of charge:
>The Bodleian Library, Oxford.
>The University Library, Cambridge.
>The National Library of Scotland, Edinburgh.
>The National Library of Wales.
>The Library of Trinity College, Dublin.

For these five copies, wait until you receive an official request from the libraries' agent. The request will come from:

>A.T. Smail, Agent,
>100 Euston Street,
>London NW1 2HQ

>Tel. No. 0171 388 5061 (when telephoning ask for Book Enquiries).

6.4.2 Copyright

Copyright is not an easy issue. The laws surrounding it are more complex than one might expect. Do not plagiarise other peoples' works; it is unethical and will hurt your reputation. Flagrant copying may result in you being sued for infringement of copyright. Most authors will not mind a brief mention, either as an acknowledgement or citation - it may, after all, boost their esteem or even sales (see *Reproducing copyrighted material* in Chapter 4).

Registering your book for copyright is achieved by depositing your book at the British library but it us not their responsibility to uphold your copyright. Some areas are obviously more sensitive than others - music scores, for example. This starts to overlap with issues regarding performance rights, etc.

If you are worried about infringement of your own copyright... it is best not to get too concerned. If you produce a reference manual or something that is of wide use or interest, it may well be photocopied without your permission. You can try to deter this by a strongly worded 'infringement of copyright' clause in the front or back of your book. You can also use your headers and footers to good effect - making it obvious where any photocopied material came from! If copying of your work without permission is blatant with no acknowledgement, then you have every right to defend your rights in the courts.

Copyright: How long does it last?
Until recently, in the UK, copyright applied for the lifetime of the author(s) plus 50 years. After the death of the author, copyright ownership is transferred to the

writer's estate. Recently, however, the 50 year rule has been extended to 70 years, following changes by the EU.

Letters and other material

In law, copyright is applied to any hand-written or typed work, regardless of whether or not it has been published formally. Copyright also applies to a speech or lecture - providing it is recorded either on paper or even a tape recorder. In the case of letters, even though the recipient may own the letter, the writer retains the copyright. Upon the death of the writer, copyright passes to his or her estate. Biographers should be beware of the change from 50 to 70 years after death rule as, just when you thought the 50 years were up, you may now have to wait another 20 if you wish to avoid seeking permission from the author's estate!

Libel

The old gung-ho attitude of "Publish and be Damned" may have had some romantic appeal in the past but unless you know what you are doing and are intimately familiar with the legal niceties - DON'T. It can be very costly. Some prominent lawyers make a half-decent living out of fighting libel cases. Be warned! Even if you have completely fictitious characters in your plot, it would be more than wise checking for any living namesakes. You may be blissfully unaware that the wicked Lord Rolpolderoll actually exists in real life - until a writ arrives on your doormat. To be safe, check in all the obvious places - Burke's Peerage, Who's Who, etc.

7. Preparing For Production

7.1 Visit your Local Printer

Unless you are planning to do *everything* yourself, visit your local printer/ printing bureau at an early stage in your venture. They are always keen for extra business and you will probably find that they are able to offer competitive prices for the services that you cannot, or do not intend to do yourself. Explain to them what you are trying to do, the kind of budget that you have to work with and the timescales that you are working to. They should be able to help with the following services:

- Cover design and printing.
- Bulk photo-copying/ laser printing.
- Binding and trimming.
- Brochures/ Flyers.
- ..and for the less intrepid, a complete typesetting, printing and binding service for your manuscript.

7.2 Hardback or Paperback

Hardback

Hardback covers are an expensive option and come in a variety of forms. If you can justify the costs and pass them on to buyers, all well and good. If your publication is of the low-volume, high value variety, then this may be the choice for you. Consult with your local printer, or look up Book Binders in the Yellow Pages directory of services to obtain estimates of costs and job turnaround times. There are often printers and binders in university towns whose stock-in-trade is binding theses for post-graduates. They may well have spare capacity and be able to satisfy short runs of hardback binding. For higher levels of production, you will need to find a commercial printer/ binder.

Paperback

Most small publishers will opt for some kind of paperback cover. Your local printer/ design bureau will be able to advise appropriate materials for your intended publication. You should discuss such issues as weight, colour and texture of the card; the finish is also important. It is a good idea to find an existing book which has a cover type that you like; show it to the printer to see if it is practicable for your kind of publication. However, be warned, technical jargon will abound, and you should be prepared for all manner of technical objections to be raised!

7.3 Cover Design

Good cover design is very important as it creates a first impression. This is especially so if your book is going to be sold through bookshops or similar outlets where potential buyers may be initially attracted by the look and feel of the cover. The recent phenomenal success of R.L.Stine's "Goosebumps" series of horror story books for children may partly be attributed to the unique covers that feature raised bumps on the surface. Like any other type of product, packaging quality and good design do count. Start planning the design well in advance of your anticipated launch date as design and production of the covers will take some time. This process can be going on in the background while other activities are underway.

The design apart, actual production of the book covers is one of the few processes that the self-publisher is not really able to do without help as the necessary equipment is large and prohibitively expensive. You will need specialist help to transfer a completed design on to a printing medium and to produce them in bulk.

7.3.1 Further details for paperback cover production

Dimensions
If you are considering an A4 format, the overall size of the unfolded cover will be 2 x A4 plus the dimensions of the spine. If you are ordering your covers sometime before completing your manuscript, you will need to take an educated guess at the thickness of the printed pages to determine the width of the spine.

Obviously, this depends on the number of pages and the type of paper you will be using.

Material
A heavy duty cartridge paper or card will normally suffice. If your book is likely to experience more rigorous than normal handling (e.g. school textbooks), then a thicker card would be advisable. Discuss these matters with your printers but do bear in mind any extra cost implications!

Finish
Card comes in a variety of finishes. The cover of our first books had a satin finish, which looked and felt good when fresh but tended to become marked after handling. We changed to a glossy finish, in common with most other paperbacks. This finish not only has a good feel but is less prone to marking and can be wiped clean. The durable gloss is achieved by a lamination process in which a covering of thin plastic film is bonded on to the exterior surface of paper. Laminating the covers will cost a bit extra and add extra time to the process but is well worth it.

7.3.2 The front cover
The front cover is one of the most important components of the book - especially so if being distributed through bookshops. If you have a design in mind, sketch out a mock-up of your ideas. You may even be able to able to use your DTP or other PC tools to produce the artwork and graphics. Discuss your preliminary ideas with your local printer/ design bureau who will be able to advise how best to present them or suggest more refined alternatives. Simple, clear designs are usually the best. Remember you are trying to catch the eye. If you are looking for something distinctive and striking but only have very limited funds to pay a designer, then it might be worth contacting a local Art/ Design college. You may well find talented final year students who would be only too pleased to earn a small commission and have their talent recognised.

The print trade uses several methods for professional colour printing. In general, the more colours you use, the more costly the cover will be. Volume production does lower the unit cost but it is as well to discuss costs early on in the process. Remember that producing covers does take some time (design, set-up, printing, laminating, trimming and folding) so it is advisable to get the cover organised some weeks in advance of the completion of your manuscript.

7.3.3 Using the back cover
You should make good use of the back cover. If it is a reference book or instruction manual, then a brief résumé of the contents is useful. This can be done by making bullet points of the main topics covered; you can also include a

few words about the authority of the author(s), e.g. "John Smith is a consultant engineer with wide experience of the nuclear power industry". A succinct summary may sway indecision and help promote a sale. If you can, include features that constitute your "unique selling proposition" (see under marketing). Note that, if the book is to be packaged in a 'shrink wrap' film, the outer covers may be the only part of the book that the customer sees. Do consider how best to use this prime advertising space.

ISBN and Barcodes

REMEMBER to put your ISBN number in the bottom right hand corner of the back cover. If you sell your books through an agency or retail outlet, consider incorporating a barcode. A barcode with your ISBN number can easily be obtained and incorporated into the back cover design - see the source list of addresses in the Appendix.

The Barcode

Barcodes have become ubiquitous with the selling process as virtually everything you buy through a retail outlet is now labelled with a barcode. When read by a special barcode reader, the barcode on supermarket goods is translated into stock item number, price and other details; for books, the barcode is usually a little simpler. As a minimum, it represents an encoded form of the ISBN number and is used by publishers, distributors and bookshops primarily for stock control. At the checkout till it is often used for automatic pricing and EPOS (Electronic Point of Sale) recording. Be warned, many major book sellers insist on having the barcode with the ISBN on the back cover.

ISBN 0-9526043-2-9

9 780952 604327

Barcode Format

For the non-technically minded, suffice it to say that a specialist supplier can produce a barcode for you in the medium of your choice (e.g. a .tif file). Give them your ISBN number and your remittance and they can return you a barcode image on a floppy disk file within a day or so (see suppliers at the end of this book). The image can then be incorporated into your back cover design. For those who are curious about barcodes and who might like to have a crack at one themselves - read on...

📖 You will need a barcode generation package, (e.g. 'Labels Unlimited' approximately £40 + VAT in the UK - see Appendix). This is more than twice the cost of getting a barcode company to print one for you and so is only worth it if you are going to be publishing two or more books or you have further use for generating barcodes or other kinds of labels.

📖 You need to determine the number for the barcode. There are various barcode formats. Fortunately, the ISBN system is of long standing and uses the barcode standard called 'European Article Numbering 13' or EAN 13, for short. This is largely equivalent to the American 'Universal Product Code'(UPC). Not the exclusive preserve of books, EAN 13 requires 13 digits of code, the first three of which, by convention are '978'. The remaining digits are specific to the individual ISBN.

To determine the number to be converted to your barcode :
1) Delete the last digit of the ISBN that you have been allocated.
2) Prefix the remaining digits with 978 (universally, the ISBN prefix).
3) Calculate a 'Check digit' using the following method:
   a) Starting with the right-most digit add up all the alternate digits reading from right to left.
   b) Multiply the result of a) by 3.
   c) Add up all the digits excluded in step a).
   d) Add the result of b) with the result of c).
   e) The check digit you require is the smallest number that, when added to the result of d) gives you a number exactly divisible by 10.

Still with it? Here's an example, take our own ISBN (see back cover) 09526043 2 9. We first drop the trailing 9 then prefix 978 giving a starting point of 978095260432 then:
   a) $2 + 4 + 6 + 5 + 0 + 7 = 24$
   b) $24 \times 3 = 72$
   c) $3 + 0 + 2 + 9 + 8 + 9 = 31$
   d) $72 + 31 = 103$
   e) $103 + 7 = 110$ ...... <u>7 is our check digit</u>

Our barcode number, including check digit is 978095260432 <u>7</u>

Barcode Sizing
The size, or magnification of the barcode on the back cover, should conform to strict limits and the 'aspect ratio', that is the ratio of height to width should be maintained. Generally, a magnification range of 80% to 200% of normal size is acceptable.

7.4 The Spine

The spine occupies the thickness of the book and is the only part of your publication that is visible amongst other books on a shelf. Make good use of it. A simple, clear title with the author (if there is room) is all that is required but if you can, make it stand out from the crowd, e.g. by using an enlarged and emboldened font.

7.5 Binding and Trimming (Paperback Books)

7.5.1 Perfect binding

Binding is another area rich in technical terms (perfect bound, stitched, etc.). Check in advance on the kind of binding that is both practicable and suitable for your publication. Most paperback books now use the 'perfect binding' method employing thermoplastic glue which adheres the pages to the inside cover along the spine. The glue is heated until semi-liquid and applied along the spine of the inside cover. The pages are pressed into the cover that folds around the pages. When cooled, the adhesive bonds pages and cover together and the now-formed books are then trimmed using a heavy-duty guillotine to give even edges. The gluing materials used these days are tough and long lasting and, providing the number of pages is not too great, the chance of your book falling apart through normal use is very low. The minimum number of pages that this method can accommodate is about 40 but there does not appear to be any particular upper limit.

For those self-publishers who will be doing the bulk printing themselves, we recommend perfect binding for loose sheets either from laser printer or photocopier. Be warned, although this method is very common and used for most modern paperbacks, magazines, etc., it can be difficult to find a printer/ binder prepared to do short runs at low unit cost. You will need to shop around. In our experience, buying the equipment for perfect binding is a costly business and not practicable for low production runs. Not only is the gluing machinery expensive but you will also need a heavy duty guillotine for trimming the books for clean square edges - another heavy and expensive piece of equipment.

7.5.2 Alternatives to perfect binding

Apart from cover printing, the perfect binding process is about the only production process that self-publishers cannot practicably achieve without expensive specialised equipment. For this reason, you may like to consider alternatives that require only office-style equipment to finish your product. For ideas on this topic, it is worth visiting one of the major stationery/ office equipment stores or contacting a mail-order supplier for a catalogue.

Although some of the alternative methods may, at first glance, give a less than professional appearance, they can be used to great effect for technical documents, e.g. reports, data-source books and training manuals. They can be seen as giving a more personalised, less mass produced feel and counter-intuitively, you may actually be able to charge more for this format! Remember that it will be for the information content that the publication will be bought - not necessarily for aesthetic 'feel'.

Here are some other binding methods we are familiar with:

📖 ***Wire staples*** For small booklets (see Booklet Printing) of up to about 72 pages in length, consider conventional stapling at the centre pages. The staples hold together both the pages and the cover. This is a very cheap means of binding as the materials required cost next to nothing. All that is needed is a long armed stapler to reach to the middle of the book and a guillotine to trim the edges square. This method is most suited to low priced books and guides.

> If your book is selling information, techniques, ideas, instructions etc., buyers will not be put off by paper quality or binding method - use what you feel is appropriate and / or cost effective.

📖 ***Ring Binders*** For reports and manuals, consider ring binders. Use the kind in which a cover page can be inserted at the front under transparent plastic. Four or more rings are much better than the standard two. Unfortunately, this method does make it easy for unauthorised photocopying, as pages can easily be removed; you could try to jog the conscience by placing the © on the header or footer of each page. Although hole punching is cheap, the cost of good quality ring binders are approximately £2-£3 each (depending on quantity ordered) plus the cost of personalised cover inserts. This method is more suited to quite high value products. Note that 'kits', such as training packs, may also include some extras such as look-up charts, CD-ROMs, computer diskettes, etc. [*Note that this kind of publication sells for premium prices*.]

📖 ***Wire comb bindings*** - Using a special combined punch and binding machine (£160-£500), small holes are punched along the spine edge of a document and a wire comb inserted and closed through the holes. A stiff cover can be inserted front and back. Alternatively, an all-in-one cover can be used with a bit of guile. This will enclose the book entirely and give you a card spine upon which you can put text. This binding that might, to some, seem rather cheap and tacky, is ideal for manuals, recipe books and field guides where it is useful to have the open pages lie completely flat on a horizontal surface.

Tip: Books that open flat. Nowadays, most writing is done directly into PC word processors and DTP. If you are using paper-based, look-up and source material for research, it is a rare joy to use books that lie open and flat unaided on the desk (made with ring binders or wire combs). As you may have already discovered, trying to type into a PC and read simultaneously from a conventionally bound book can be difficult. Without using your hands, the pages have to be kept open with weights or other contrivances! If you are going to publish a source/ data book which readers will be referring to whilst typing or other manual tasks (e.g., cooking), do consider ring binders and wire comb bindings. There are two other major advantages:
- Manufacturing books using these binding methods can be done at home and give you the freedom to make them as and when they are required - without relying on the services of outside printers/ binders.
- This being so, you need carry only a small amount of stock - you can manufacture to order.

7.6 Bulk Printing

For printing books for paying customers, three processes were mentioned in the Introduction: photocopying, laser printing and the conventional print process. There are a number of factors that may influence which printing process will suit you best:

📖 The number of copies that you estimate you will require initially.

- The number of pages in your publication.
- The money that you have for investment in your project.
- The quality that you require or would find acceptable.
- The time-scale to which you are working.

Below we summarise relative costs and benefits of each method The costs are approximate and are based on 1997 prices.

7.6.1 Laser printing method

Initial capital Cost: Laser Printer £300-£1500 depending on type

Unit Costs		
(pence per side)	[1]A4 Paper	0.5p
	[2]Toner	1.5p
	[3]Depreciation	0.2p
	[4]Overheads	0.2p
	Total	**2.4p**

[1]Based upon £5 per 500 sheets (1000 sides)
[2]Based upon 5000 side coverage at £75 per toner cartridge
[3]Based upon an initial cost of £400 and a 200,000 page life and
[4]Estimate for maintenance, labour, electricity, etc.

Cost of printing a typical A4 size book of 180 pages = £0.024 x 180 = £4.32
..and an A5 size book of 180 pages = £4.32 / 2 = £2.16

On these estimates, we would expect the laser to print 1100 A4 books or 2200 A5 books before needing replacement or a major overhaul (allowed for by using a depreciation factor).

For relatively small print runs, this represents a very viable option.

Advantages:
- The outlay on a printer may be offset by other printing requirements.
- The quality will be good (probably 600dpi resolution).
- The unit costs are fixed - but remember to include a factor to depreciate the cost of the printer based on its estimated lifetime.
- You can print copies on demand.
- You are able to make small textual corrections at will.

Disadvantages:
- Fairly labour intensive (DIY).
- Relatively slow, e.g. 6-12ppm (for mid-range printers), so 180 A4 pages will take 15-30 minutes to print (7.5 - 15 minutes for A5 format).

   📖 Unless you have a duplex printer, you will need to reverse the paper manually to print on the opposite side. This is more time consuming and some wastage may occur.

   📖 Restricted to using an A4 source of paper (unless you can afford an A3 printer.

'Booklet Printing' Most lasers can only print up to an A4 size (standard for the UK). A3 (twice the size of A4) printers are available but much more costly. Producing books of a smaller size than A4 is likely to be wasteful in paper as trimming will be required. However, some DTP packages, e.g. PageMaker, facilitate 'Booklet' printing. This method allows you to print multiple pages on one sheet of paper. For example, two A5 format pages can be printed side by side on a sheet of A4. If your DTP does not include booklet printing options (like Microsoft Word) - all is not lost as some printers include 'add-on' formatting software, (e.g. NEC 860 Superscript). You may like to bear this in mind when selecting your DTP and/or printer. Alternatively, it is possible to obtain add-on software that facilitates booklet and 'n-up' printing which will work for most printer types (see the web site for Forefront's ClickBook product).

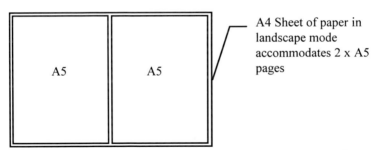

A4 Sheet of paper in landscape mode accommodates 2 x A5 pages

Booklet printing software can rearrange page sequences to allow centre stapling. For example, for an A5 booklet comprising 50 pages printed on two A5 pages per side of A4, the page sequencing for the outermost sheet will be:

on one side   on the reverse

         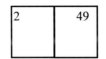

The next sheet will have the sequence:

   48   3   4   47

In practice, there is no limit to how many pages there are in a 'booklet'. There are also other printing methods to enable multiple pages to be printed on a sheet of paper ('n up' printing).

7.6.2 Photocopying printing method (using a bureau)

This method requires the least outlay. You need to produce a high quality 'master copy' which can be printed on a relatively low priced ink/bubblejet or laser printer. A printer with better than 300dpi resolution is recommended.

| Initial Costs | Low priced printer (assuming that you are not purchasing the photocopier). |
| Unit Cost | Photocopying: typical bureau costs are £0.06 - £0.08 per double-sided of A4 copy. |

Printing cost for a 180 page A4 book = £5.40 - £7.20 (for A5 = £2.70 - £3.60)

Advantages
- 📖 Low capital outlay on equipment (e.g. bubblejet for master copy).
- 📖 Not mutually exclusive of the laser printing method.
- 📖 No labour (=time) involvement for you.
- 📖 No wastage, the printer bureau only charges for good copies.
- 📖 You are able to make small textual corrections at will (between runs).

Disadvantages
- 📖 Higher unit cost than own laser printing.
- 📖 You need to maintain rigorous quality control as photocopy quality can vary between and within batches.
- 📖 You are committed to using an A4 source of paper (same comments as laser printing).

7.6.3 Conventional printing process

This process differs from the first two in two significant ways:
- 📖 The unit cost depends on the number of books to be printed as part of the cost includes the initial set-up charges. The larger the print run, the greater the economies of scale and the lower the unit cost as the set-up charges per copy diminish proportionately.

- 📖 The printing company can, if required, handle the whole book production process: printing, cover binding, trimming and, if required, packaging (e.g. shrink wrapped polythene).

Estimating costs, therefore, becomes a little more difficult. Using the same imaginary 180 page book in A4 format, the following costs are a realistic guide:

| Initial Costs | The first print run necessarily includes set-up costs. A run of 1000 copies might costs as much as £4000 (£4 per copy - including covers, binding and trimming) but the unit cost |

falls with the size of the run as the set-up charges are diluted. 5,000 copies might cost £10,000 (£2 per copy). Set-up charges may be much less if the printers can use your type-setting taken from a compatible file supplied by you from your DTP package.

Subsequent Costs   'Run-ons', and reprinting from the previously prepared plates, will not incur the same set-up costs. A run-on of, say, 5,000 could cost as little as £8,000 (£1.60 per copy).

So we can estimate the cost of printing a typical 180 page book as £1.60 to £4 (complete) depending on the amount work required for the set-up and the size of the print run.

Advantages
- 📖 Economies of scale - the least unit cost, therefore, potentially the highest profit.
- 📖 Hassle free - the Printers complete the whole process.
- 📖 Consistent product with high degree of quality control.
- 📖 Labour free to the publisher.

Disadvantages
- 📖 Requires substantial initial outlay (£1000's).
- 📖 Dry, spacious storage accommodation needed for your stock.
- 📖 No opportunity to correct minor errors (except between print runs).
- 📖 Requires forward planning as the printers will need to be booked well in advance.
- 📖 Could be left with substantial 'remainders' if unable to sell your stock.

7.7 Paper Quality

Paper type and quality that you require depends on your chosen printing method and needs careful consideration. Paper prices vary enormously so you should strike a balance between cost and quality. The following points should be considered:

7.7.1 Paper for laser printers and photocopying
Use a good quality paper, both in finish and in weight. For office machinery, (lasers, photocopiers, etc.) paper thickness is specified by weight in gsm (gm. per m^2). Run-of-the-mill photocopy and laser printer paper is usually 75-80gsm and of intermediate economy-grade quality. For books, however, you should use good quality paper, usually of 90-100 gsm. Quality varies tremendously. In particular, look for these other factors:

Colour: Most books are printed on slightly off-white paper which is easier on the eye than pure white. Many 'business' quality papers are pure white which can look rather sharp - do some research with paper suppliers if you feel this is a significant factor.

Texture: Some cheaper papers have a fibrous texture and give poorer print quality.

Translucence: If you intend to include many diagrams or photographic images, dense print will show through the other side if the paper is too thin or translucent.

Grain: Paper has a 'grain' that causes it to be more pliable in one direction than another. For most office-type A4 paper, the grain runs parallel to the long axis so pages are more pliable when turning them in portrait mode (taller than wide). If you intend to produce A5 books by printing two A5 pages per A4 sheet in portrait mode (see 7.6.1), the grain on your cut pages will run horizontally instead of vertically. Perfect bound (i.e. a rigid, glued spine), A5 books manufactured in this way, may offer significantly more resistance to page turning and snap shut! So do investigate the grain properties of paper before ordering in bulk!

Bulk: This is the volume of the paper. Weight is not the only factor in determining the thickness of the paper as densities can vary. Bulk is normally measured in pages per inch (ppi). If you know the ppi of your paper and the number of pages you are likely to need, you can calculate the final thickness of your book - a useful statistic when specifying dimensions for covers and binding.

Cost: You will find tremendous variation in price so, if you choose one of the more expensive papers, check your projected costs before ordering in quantity. [Note that the costings given for laser printing show the most significant cost item is laser toner not paper].

Curling characteristics: Laser printers and photocopiers fuse toner powder to paper at a temperature of about 200°C. The effect of heating and the passage through the roller mechanism will cause paper to curl. Different papers will have a variable susceptibility to curling, but generally the thicker the paper, the greater the curl. This can cause problems in the finished product but of greater significance is the difficulty in printing on the reverse side if not using a duplex printer. The greater the curl, the less satisfactory it will be for producing books.

If you want to use a 90gsm weight or above, you may need to use more expensive 'bond' paper which is not so prone to curling.

 Read the instructions for your laser printer / photocopier carefully before ordering paper in bulk. Most laser printers specify the characteristics and tolerances of paper quality that should be used. Some factors, such as abrasiveness and thickness of paper, will affect the working life of major printer components through wear and tear. Stationers and paper suppliers should be able to give the manufacturer's ratings for factors such as suitability for laser printing, duplex printing etc. Check that the paper you wish to use is suitable for your purpose and equipment before buying in quantity.

If you intend to manufacture the books yourself, either by laser printing or photocopying, experiment with different types of paper to determine the optimum for factors such as 'look and feel', cost and practicability. Unless you produce trial copies, it is possible to overlook factors in the manufacturing process that may confound your plans. For example, the binding process you intend to use may limit the possible minimum and maximum thickness of the book. The thickness of the paper may, therefore, be a significant factor if approaching either threshold. Low weight or low quality paper may result in waviness in and between the pages, giving an unsatisfactory result. A few experimental prototypes, including the binding process should iron out any difficulties.

Speak to your office stationery supplier or print bureau who may be able to provide invaluable advice and possibly a range of sample materials for you to try. When you have chosen a suitable type of paper they will probably be able to offer a discount because they normally buy in bulk and will have negotiated substantial discounts with suppliers. As with any business, keep your unit costs as low as possible to maximise your profits.

7.7.2 Paper selection for conventional printing

Selection of paper for books printed by conventional printing methods (e.g. off-set litho) requires a different approach. Here, you will need to liase more closely with a printing bureau as other factors are involved. For example, a number of book pages will be printed simultaneously on much larger sheets of paper (called the signature). Ideally, the number of printed pages in your book should have a multiple of the signature, i.e. use complete sheets so that no paper is wasted. For example, if the signature is 16 pages per sheet, ideally your book should have 16, 32, 48, 64, 80 or 96, etc. pages for optimum economy. There are many kinds of paper available and it is a matter of choice and cost. If you intend to use photographs, you will probably require inserts of a higher quality paper; discuss this with your local print bureau and cost out the various options available to you.

7.7.3 An incremental process

To maximise your profit from publishing, you should be looking for the lowest unit production costs. Of the three options discussed, the conventional ink-on-paper print run is the obvious choice for maximising profit as costs can be in the order of a half to a third of the laser/photocopy method. The snag, of course, is the money you will need to find 'up front'. Let's suppose you do not have sufficient funds to commit to this process and you are hoping to fund production largely from sales. For the following example, we have estimated for a 180 page, A4 size book with a proposed selling price of £15 per copy. The table below details the fall in production costs as we progress from method to method:

*Production Costs	Selling Price	Margin Over Production Costs
1) Photocopy method, first 100 copies at £8.00 each	£15	£15.00 - £8.00 = £7.00
2) Photocopy method, subsequent 100s : £6.95 each	£15	£15.00 - £6.95 = £8.05
3) Laser printing method: £5.42 each	£15	£15.00 - £5.42 = £9.58
4) Conventional offset litho: run of first 1000 : £4000 (£4.50 each)	£15	£15.00 - £4.00 = £11.00 Includes initial set-up costs
5) Subsequent 1000s : £1900 (£1.90 each)	£15	£15.00 - £1.90 = £13.10

*The costs quoted include covers and binding. Note that VAT may or may not be levied for photocopying services: Books are currently free of VAT in the UK but printing services may not be.

A sensible production strategy

Unless you are extremely optimistic or have a sure market for your product, it is perhaps a wise strategy to 'test the water'. Unless you are certain you can sell 1000 copies easily, you could produce 50 copies of your book using a photocopy process (Option 1) or laser (Option 3). Assuming you had a 180 page book, this would cost you either £400 or £271, (it could be more or less, depending on the size of the book.) If you are able to sell these copies easily, you can continue with the same process until you feel sufficiently confident to invest in a greater quantity and proceed to Option 4. If you can sell into multiple 1000s you could be 'in clover' with Option 5. Of course, if you use Option 1 and don't sell many books, your outlay is relatively small and you won't have your spare room full of unsaleable stock!

Another major benefit of the photocopy and laser printing method for initial production is the facility to correct any minor blemishes - spelling mistakes, punctuation, etc. If you go straight to the high volume printing option you will not have an opportunity to make any corrections.
And, if you are financially constrained or do not wish to take risks unnecessarily, you can use your 'profits' from options 1) and 2) to fund the full print run with the confidence that you will be able to continue or even increase sales.

7.7.4 Transferring your book to an offset-litho process

If the printing process changes and your book retains the same content (other than minor corrections to the text), you will be able to use the same ISBN number. If, however, your book changes in content, you will need to issue a new edition or revision. This must be noted in the frontispiece, and you will need to use a new ISBN number (remembering of course, to advise Whitaker's three months in advance).
You should also aim to avoid having your Printers (print bureau) retype and typeset the whole book again in their own publishing software. This will avoid both delay and extra cost. There are two principle methods to achieve this:

1) Transferring your document to a Print Bureau's Publishing Package

A print bureau may be able to take your document in its entirety, import it into their own publishing package and from here be able to create the master 'plates' on their own machinery. This may then only require a minimum of further preparatory work (and cost to you). Check in advance that this route is possible and that your DTP package is either compatible with theirs or it is easily converted to a compatible format which they can read. If it is not possible, they may be able to advise you of someone who can undertake converting documents from one package to another.

2) Encapsulated PostScript (EPS) Files

This is an alternative approach in which the print bureau may be able to take a disk file containing a print output file and direct it to their own device. You create the file by selecting the 'print to file' option on your print set-up instead of directing the output to your inkjet or laser device. You will probably need to use a 'PostScript' type printer 'driver'. A PostScript (EPS) file can be read by any PostScript printer and hence is a convenient means of print output exchange.You may have a PostScript printer (especially if you are using Apple equipment). They are generally more expensive because of the extra sophistication they need to translate the EPS instructions. If you have not got a PostScript printer, all is not lost because your Windows 3.x or Windows 95 set-up disks will contain drivers for various types of PostScript printers. The following instructions may be helpful in creating an EPS file in these circumstances:

1. Load a suitable driver into your print manager (consult your Windows manual if you do not know how).
2. **Make a copy of your current document.**
3. Select the newly loaded postscript printer (driver) in the print set-up option in your DTP and click on 'OK'. The DTP will now reformat your pages in line with the new printer driver.
4. There will inevitably be slight differences in the format of your copy document because of small differences in dimensions from your normal printer device and adjustments will be required.
5. If there are more lines per page than previously, you can correct it by altering the page layout dimensions slightly OR by judiciously inserting a blank line here and there to pad out the document so it appears the same as previously.
6. If there are fewer lines per page than previously, it may be possible to remove the odd blank line or slightly increase the printing area of the page by reducing the size of the bottom margin.
7. If you cannot get the pages in the same place as they were previously, your Table of Contents will come adrift of the page numbers, and so will the Index. It must be adjusted so Index and TOC page number references remain synchronised. If this cannot be achieved, then both TOC and Index will need to be regenerated.
8. Finally, preview the print to check that the output is as you expect it to be, then direct output to a disk file as described above.
9. The resultant file may thence be given to the print bureau for processing!

Tip: If you have a file of a greater size than a conventional 3.5", 1.44Mb floppy disk and you want to transfer it from your PC to another (e.g. a PostScript print file) or just want to make a back-up copy, you may be able to compress it. PKZIP is a utility that can achieve a compression ratio of up to 5:1. Thus, if you have a file of 5Mb, it may be possible to compress it to as little as 1Mb as a .zip file. When transferred to another PC, it may be uncompressed to its normal size (using PKUNZIP). If the compressed file still exceeds the 1.44Mb capacity, no problem, the compression utility has an option to write to multiple (sequential) floppy disks.

Remember, If you are intending to use this incremental route to printing, check out the whole process with your printing bureau before producing your first books. Specifically:

📖 Ask the printers if they can import whole documents from your DTP package; if they can, then major retyping and reformatting can be avoided.

📖 OR whether they can accept an EPS file to create the printing 'plates' directly for, say, an off-set litho press.

📖 Ensure that you can faithfully reproduce the page layouts using different printer drivers.

📖 Cost out your strategy. You will need to know at what point it becomes worth transferring to a conventional print process. Find out how long this process will take. It could take 3-6 weeks to achieve, depending on how busy your print bureau is and whether any retyping is required.

8. Marketing And Sales

📖 *Who are your potential customers?*
📖 *How do you tell them you exist?*

You now have to change roles from being a writer/ editor to a marketing/ advertising executive. It does not matter how valuable a contribution you have made to your chosen field, unless you can 'connect' with an appreciative audience your work will remain unknown. Now is the time for real creative thinking - how can you effectively bring your book to the attention of potential buyers? Unless you have created an entirely new niche, you will be in competition with other eager authors and publishers most of whom will have far greater resources and marketing experience than yourself.

If you have created something of value (either useful or entertaining), be assured that there will customers out there to buy it. You should by now have gone through a peer review process. Unless you chose sycophants to review your work at pre-publication stage, you will have had some kind of objective feedback about your creation.

8.1 Marketing Principles

If you have no experience of marketing, we strongly suggest you visiting a major library or bookshop to do some research on the subject. You will find no shortage of advice. There is an enormous range of books on the subject as there are many different approaches to this topic covering the gamut of products and services. The self-publisher has the difficult task of breaking into a crowded market with probably only a very limited budget and so some basic understanding of marketing principles will give focus to this endeavour. The publishing business is a very specialised one with its own methods and intricacies; below we detail a few of the marketing principles that apply to the marketing process in general.

8.1.1 Unique Selling Proposition (USP)

First, you must decide why people would want to buy your particular product as opposed to somebody else's. In marketing terms, does your product have a 'Unique Selling Proposition' that marks it out from the competition (if there is any competition)? Let's take the position of you as publisher of a specialist technical book which might not have much more to offer than others on the same subject. In other words, no USP. Why should people want to buy your book rather than the others? Here are several possible reasons:

- Price   Its cheaper than the opposition.
- Quality   It has higher standards of presentation and finish.
- Advertising You are more effective at gaining the attention of potential buyers.
- Availability Your book is more readily available.

As a small publisher, perhaps wrestling with production quality, distribution and high unit costs, you will find it difficult to beat other, more established publishers on any of the above terms. *Therefore, we would strongly recommend that you bear in mind the principle of Unique Selling Proposition when you are writing your book.* In practical terms, this means putting some distance between you and your rivals or finding a niche where there is limited or no competition. If there are already comparable books on the subject, study them closely and make sure that yours is in some way separated from the crowd by being:

- More comprehensive.
- More accurate.
- More up to date.
- Broader appeal by covering additional subject matter.
- Better written - more 'sparkle'.

If you cannot find a way of 'out performing' other books in direct competition for your readership, then consider broadening the appeal of your book. By doing this you may be able to increase the potential customer base. For example, in this book we describe a proven method by which small self-publishers can use the Internet to build an international market for a very small financial outlay. In fact, the same methods will apply to any new small business with specialist products. Thus, we hope this book will attract some buyers from other kinds of small businesses, not necessarily connected with publishing, who wish to create extra international business. Although Internet marketing is not the main theme of the book, it will have value to other kinds of business. Its appeal, therefore, has been broadened beyond those who may just be determining the feasibility of self-publishing. Another example might be in the area of teaching. If your subject appears in a school or college curriculum, this point can be developed, perhaps with cross references to other curriculum-based textbooks. Your book thereby becomes a useful resource for teachers, lecturers or students- hence increasing your book's marketability.

8.1.2 Market Analysis

Who will be most interested in buying your book? Can you classify potential buyers by market sector(s)? This process will have great bearing on your advertising. Let us suppose again that you have published a reference-type book. Where will the widest appeal be?

Market	Examples of Book Subjects
Local	Local History, Stories & Legends, Buildings, Walks, Recipes, Famous People, etc.
Regional	Local topics plus subjects with wider appeal, e.g. Geography, Industry, Architecture and Dialect.
National	Topics with wide appeal such as Biography, Novels, Poetry, Humour, English Language, School curriculum, Sport and General Interest.
International	Topics of appeal not specific to any one country, e.g. Archaeology, Economics, Specialist Subjects, Travel, Marketing.
Specialist or Niche Market	Computing, Economics, Science, Philosophy, Science Fiction, 'Ologies', Education, Market Intelligence.

Clearly these markets overlap. Subjects for local and regional markets group together, as do those that are of national, international and specialist interest. Deciding which group(s) your publication best falls into is a pre-cursor to formulating your marketing policy.

Market Size

Just because you have identified an international market for your publication, it does not necessarily mean a mass market. Similarly, niche, local or regional markets are not necessarily small. If your potential market is say, 2 million (county or region) and you managed to sell to 0.1% (1 in a 1000) that still represents 2000 sales. If your profit margin is £10 per copy that represents £20,000 profit.

Repeat Market

Although your market may be small, you may be lucky in being able to tap into a repeat market. For example, if you publish a sourcebook for data that rapidly goes out of date, you may be able to count on customers re-ordering new revisions on an annual basis to keep up to date with current information (e.g., *The Writer's Handbook* published annually). Alternatively, if your work is used in the educational/ academic world as a recommended student text you can expect fresh orders each year as new students purchase the recommended reading for coursework.

8.2 Pricing

This is a very important topic and you will need to do some careful analysis before deciding a sensible pricing policy. The following points outline a good approach to setting a price for your book:

- Put yourself in the place of a potential buyer. If it is a source book for information or data, how valuable would this be to you and how much would you be willing to pay?
- Are there any comparable publications in the same subject area? If so, how are they priced? Unless your work is much superior, it would seem unwise to price your product much above the competition.
- How much did it cost to produce? You would be a little foolish to price at below your production costs other than for promotional purposes.
- Take all your other costs into consideration: advertising, packaging, distribution and wastage. (Initially, at least, you are unlikely to resist giving copies to friends, relatives and acquaintances and you will probably send copies off to magazines and journals for editors to review.)

For the publishing industry a good rule of thumb is a retail price of not less than 5 times the production cost. For us, as small publishers, our unit production costs may be well above industry norm because of our smaller production runs. However, we hope that our margin is much higher than the industry would normally expect to achieve.

8.2.1 Pricing for specialist publications

If your publication is in the form of a report, review or technical document, different pricing factors may apply. Some specialist reports aimed, for example, at local authorities or certain other institutions, are often very highly priced. This reflects the time and expertise that was used to compile them. Buyers of these specialist publications will understand the limited nature of their distribution. Remember, therefore, that it may not only be private individuals buying your product and so cost is unlikely to be a limiting factor in sales.

For professionals such as merchant bankers or fund managers, price again is unlikely to be a constraining factor. Conversely, if you are aiming primarily for students, pensioners or others with less disposable income, no matter how valuable your product is in terms of content, pricing will be a very significant factor.

For our first book, *'A Practical Guide to Relational Database Design'*, we commented in our advertising literature that, if the methods that we advised were followed, valuable time could be saved during the design phase of a database project. Given that even modest computing projects can cost thousands of pounds per day to finance, the purchase price of our book would be recouped many times in just a few hours. Many of our customers for the database book have been companies and institutions who may well have been prepared to pay a lot more. An equal number of customers, however, have been individuals who would not have been prepared to pay much more than the cover price of £24.99! The price we chose, therefore, represented a balance.

High Volume, Low Price vs. Low Volume, High Price
Try and determine where your main market lies; construct a few pricing scenarios. For example, suppose the production costs are £8 per copy. Perhaps 25% of your market is in the corporate sector who would be prepared to pay £48 (margin £40) for a 'sourcebook'. The remaining 75% of your market are private individuals and £20 (margin £12) per copy is as much as the market will bear.

If out of 100 customers only 25 are corporate, paying £48 per copy, this would net £1200. Selling at £20 might attract all 100 customers, which also nets £1200. When you take postage, packaging, invoicing and the other sundry administrative, time-consuming tasks into consideration, it is likely that the lower sales, higher price option is the most profitable! Note also, perversely, it may be easier to sell at the higher 'exclusive' price. The message here is, understand your market and do not just go for volume.

Pricing Thresholds
Most publishers and bookshops use the old pricing threshold trick: £9.99 is psychologically more enticing a price than £10. Other thresholds are £14.99, £19.99, £24.99 and £29.99. Above this price, for books at least, the threshold effect is diminished although other points on the price scale might be effective at £49.99 and £99.99.

8.3 The Selling Process

In order to make money you have to sell books and collect the proceeds from your customers. The selling process requires careful planning as it is critical to your success or failure as a publisher. If you are not participating in a co-operative or using an agency then you must consider doing it for yourself.

8.3.1 Selling through retail outlets

Distributing directly to retail outlets is not particularly easy. You will probably find it easier using an agent or specialist buyer/supplier who has the necessary contacts and knows the market inside out. You could, potentially have a vast (though competitive) market - if the quality of your publication is high enough - and there is demand for your product BUT be prepared to lose 50-60% of the cover price along the way to wholesale and retail margins. The retailer will want a 30-35% margin and the buyers/distributors will also want their margin of 20-25% so the two together explain why you will generally receive less than 50%! However, it is still potentially profitable. Using the breakdown for Option 4) given earlier for our 180 page book as an example:

Selling price £15 (well, £14.99 really..) less 55% = £6.75
£6.75 - £1.90 (production costs) = **£4.85 profit**

Sell 1000 books (only 1 book in every 3 UK towns!) and you have £4850, and remember there are fewer hassles in the selling process, someone else will be taking the money from the public, dealing with credit cards and so on.

Many book shops work on a sale or return basis and even then you will find a fairly long invoicing cycle - so unless you have a best-seller on your hands, be prepared to play the 'long game' with retail sales.

8.3.2 Selling to Libraries

Readers of your book will either purchase a copy for themselves, or like many millions of people, borrow a copy from either a public or some other institutional library. Selling to libraries, therefore, can be a major source of income to publishers. In the UK, there are many thousands of libraries of various sorts: public, private, company, educational and others. There are over 6000 public lending libraries alone. Between them they have an enormous budget for buying books and are certainly worth targeting as a market. Most libraries buy their books through specialist library suppliers, of which there are only a few. These suppliers actively look for new titles to supply their customers and circulate trade listings to the library buyers. (Note that libraries also respond to requests from their customers - so prompt your friends and relations to request your book from their local library!). Consequently, it is well worth sending brochures and free copies to the chief buyers of the library suppliers (see under 'Useful Addresses' in the Appendix). If they like your book and they anticipate a reasonable trade with the libraries, you may well be able to tap in to this lucrative market. Why stop at the UK library market? If your book is on a specialist subject and of international appeal, try the U.S.A, where there are well over 100,000 libraries; selling to just a few per cent could be very profitable. The names and addresses of the most prominent library suppliers are given in the Appendix.

Additionally, in the UK, the Public Lending Right scheme (PLR) can provide you with a small additional income as authors are paid each time one of their books is borrowed from a public library. (*See Section 8.8*.)

8.3.3 Direct selling

If you can do it, this is the most profitable route to selling. From the cover price, you deduct the production, advertising and distribution costs and the rest (taxman, excepting) will be yours. But how do you bring your book to the attention of the public? Here's the rub! You need to advertise - and provide plenty of information to would-be buyers if you are going to sell by post - as your potential readers will not have the opportunity of leafing through the book on the shelf or bookstand.

8.4 Advertising

Advertising will probably be the most expensive aspect of the whole venture. It is also rather hit and miss as you can never tell in advance whether you will even get your money back on the cost of an advertisement. You will have to think long and hard about your target audience. A careful strategy is required for your advertising or you will waste a lot of money.

For example, suppose you want to sell on a national basis; if you were to put a small advert in a national trade journal or national newspaper what kind of costs are you likely to incur? Typically, (at the time of writing) you can expect to pay £30-£60 (+ VAT) per 'column' cm, where a 'column' is 30-40mm wide. An advert of 5 'column' centimetres might give you a box 5x4 cm. The cost, therefore, would be £200-£300 + VAT for a rather small box! Choosing this approach, you could not launch a very big campaign with only £1000. To recover such an amount, how many books would you have to sell?

8.4.1 Free advertising

There are, however, many other avenues to explore and, if you can, take advantage of as much free and inexpensive advertising as you can. If you are anticipating only a local market, your advertising costs will be a lot less. You could try your local bookshop, tourist office or building society for a window display. It is surprising how many passers by there are and, although you might only get 1 sale in 1000, it is a start!

One form of advertising worth pursuing is not really advertising at all. If your book covers a specialist subject, that is, has its own societies or professional associations (e.g. computing, astronomy, horticulture), there are likely to be periodicals, newsletters, and journals distributed to members. It can be profitable to write to the secretaries of societies and features editors with proposals for articles to be written in your specialist field. If you are lucky, you may be given a commission, in which case you can then rework extracts from your book so the task does not need to be too onerous. At the end you can put "John Smith is an independent consultant and author and may be contacted on...". You might then give your telephone number or, better still your web page address (*see WWW pages*), additionally the editor might let you quote the name and ISBN number of your book.

> **Tip:** Writing articles in specialist journals is the best form of advertising because readers know that the material is written is usually authoritative and subject to editorial control. Articles are not overt advertising but, if readers respond favourably, and would like further information they will seek further information about your book. You may also be paid a fee for writing the article! It is always worth approaching editors because, having written one article, you may be invited to write others and perhaps asked to review books etc. This can only be good for your reputation, will promote your career and hopefully boost book sales.

The Writers Handbook 1997 gives a list of professional associations, journals and associations and may prove very useful in drawing up a list of possible publications which you consider appropriate outlets for your area of expertise.

8.4.2 Local and regional press

If you live in a provincial or country area, you will undoubtedly be served by a local or regional newspaper. Advertising in a local newspaper is considerably less costly than a national one and there is often a regular spot for local authors and new ventures. Journalists are always looking for interesting stories to fill their pages. If you are publishing something of local interest, you may be able to get a small feature written about you and your book, including a photograph. This is good publicity and it is free! If you have any idiosyncrasies or eccentricities so much the better - it personalises the story! The best approach is to prepare a 'press release' and send it to the news desk or the editor. Send a covering letter, perhaps drawing on your preface for material You can make a press release in a brochure format for reuse later.

> **Tip:** Order extra copies of your book cover on glossy paper, these are inexpensive and make excellent posters for publicity purposes.

The larger regional newspapers are also worth approaching. They are still relatively inexpensive to advertise in and do have very high numbers of readers. You might also be lucky enough to get a small write-up about you and your book along the same lines as in the previous paragraph.

Preparing a brochure/ press release: a simple single page example

++ Press Release ++
New Title from Domanski-Irvine Books
Publication Date 1st July 1997

A Practical Guide to

Publishing Books
Using Your PC

Organising,
Writing,
Printing
& Marketing
Your Own Books

Peter Domanski
& Philip Irvine

Price: £12.99   ISBN 0 952 60432 9

In the last few years the wide availability of cheap and powerful personal computers has enabled authors to write, produce and publish their own books with relative ease and for very low cost. This new book takes the reader through all the steps in the publication process providing tried and tested practical advice based upon our own experience in self-publishing. We describe a variety of simple production methods and provide a number of alternative options to suit every budget. The importance of marketing is emphasised and we demonstrate effective ways of using the Internet.

⧏ *Some of the topics covered:*

⧉ What hardware you will need: PC specifications, printers etc.

⧉ What software you will need: DeskTop Publishing packages, graphics, ClipArt etc.

⧉ Planning and organising your publication. Aligning to your potential market.

⧉ Creating a 'story-board', advice for writing your book.

⧉ Selecting your book format, layout, chapter and paragraph styles.

⧉ The components of books, Table of Contents, Index etc.

⧉ The publishing process - obtaining an ISBN number, copyright considerations, legal requirements etc.

⧉ Low cost printing and production methods with full cost breakdowns for photocopying, laser printing and conventional printing options.

⧉ Book covers and binding methods.

⧉ Marketing and Sales techniques. Using the media, making effective use of your advertising budget.

⧉ Using the Internet to create national and international sales, e-mail, creating your own web site.

The book and further information may be obtained from:
Domanski-Irvine Books, Coldwell Farm, Stretfordbury, Leominster, Herefordshire, UK. (Tel/Fax 01234 567890).   See also *http://www.dibookco.u-net.com*

8.4.3 National press, journals and magazines

If your publication is of wider interest, you will need to plan your campaign with care to maximise the use of your limited budget, ideally building your advertising campaign by funding it from earnings. You can still try local newspapers, etc. but you must set your sights on national sales - your market is much wider. Given that advertising in national daily and weekly journals is very expensive and transitory, you must be discerning about where and when you advertise. For example, go for journals with a long 'shelf-life', e.g. monthly magazines. The glossy monthly magazines and journals do not cost much more than daily or weekly newspapers to advertise in. They are normally read at a more leisurely pace and many of them end up in waiting rooms where they can sit for months if not years, (look at the magazine table of your doctor's or dentist's for evidence of this).

Where you choose to advertise will also be largely dependant on the nature of your publication: 'Canals of the West Midlands' is not best suited to 'Fur and Feather'. *The Writers Handbook* gives a very full list of magazines and newspapers (regional and national). It also gives details of advertising rates and circulation figures so you will have plenty of information here for planning your advertising campaign. One way you can estimate the relative cost effectiveness of different advertising publications is to divide the advertising cost by the circulation figure. For example, a £250 advertisement in a magazine with a circulation of 50,000 means that it costs £0.005 (0.5p) to reach each reader. A similar magazine with a circulation of only 40,000, and costing £300 to advertise, costs £0.0075 per person (0.75p). The first option, therefore, appears to be the more cost effective on numbers alone. Of course, this takes no consideration of the type of readership, careful judgement is required as to which publication best represents your target audience.

8.4.4 Making the advert count

Obviously the relative position of the advertisement is important. For example, in the Sunday newspapers there are extensive sections for Business Opportunities, Personal, Services, etc. Of course there is a large potential audience, but just how eye catching will your small £400 advert be amongst the others? For around £750 (+ VAT) you could have a small advert in the Scribble Pad next to the crossword in the Daily Telegraph - which is eye catching - but can you afford to risk such a large sum? The response could be enormous but it is a big risk. £750 is probably approaching your entire capital investment in your PC equipment. If there are parts of a magazine, or journal which you think are particularly prominent or eye-catching, ask for a price from the editor. It could be money better spent than on a small box in the classified ads where people only look when they specifically want something. *Be inventive!*

114

Advertisements do not have to be large to be eye-catching but they do need to stimulate the reader to reach for his or her cheque book and place an order!

To the left is an advertisement, reproduced at natural size, that we used in several newspapers and magazines to advertise our first book. It was designed to give impact even though the size was small. It occupies one column width and is 5cm deep (space is usually sold in column cm). It was created in Microsoft Word and the circular text employed the WordArt extension. We hope that it abides by the well-known marketing principle of AIDA.

8.4.5 The AIDA principle
This acronym stands for:

- Attention   Catch the attention of your intended audience.
- Interest   Hold that attention and create interest in your product.
- Desire   Create a desire to buy the product.
- Action   Provide an action point (buy now for an introductory offer).

[Note: sometimes C, for Confidence, is inserted after Desire]

8.4.6 Advertising: discounts and payment terms
Be cheeky! Ask whether the journal offers publishers' discounts. You will probably be able to get a discount for multiple insertions, but try to find out if there are any other 'trade' discounts. Classified advertising managers are usually willing to negotiate. If they still have space to sell near their deadlines, like aircraft operators with seats to sell, they would rather sell something at a discount than for nothing at all! Also, note that most journals and magazines nowadays are in the hands of a very limited number of owners. Much of the advertising for different magazines in the same group is handled from the same office, even the same personnel. You may be able to get a discount across several different journals belonging to the same group - it's worth a try.

> **Tip:** It is well worth trying to establish an account with a publishing group. Payment term for account holders is normally 28 days. Over this length of time, you may have a significant yield from an advertisement before you actually have to pay for it - It all helps cash flow! Non-account customers are usually required to pay in advance (pre-pay) for their advertisements.

© Domanski & Irvine 1997

8.4.7 The Advertisement as an order form

To make it easier for the public to buy your book, consider incorporating an order form into your advertisements. The customer can fill in the order form, cut it out and post it off with a cheque or credit card details. This simplifies direct sales for you and your customers as the need for phone calls and hand-written orders and enquiries is minimised. When you advertise in the press, however, you should be prepared to undertake to indemnify the magazine, newspaper or journal against claims by dissatisfied customers - they have consumer rights.

To sell 'off the page', the journal's advertising editor will need to verify that you are *bona fide* and you will have to provide details of your company, trading address, bankers, etc. If you are not selling directly off the page, but inviting 'further inquiries', the advertising managers will be less stringent as direct selling is not involved.

8.4.8 Mailshots

Sending a press release, brochure or 'flyer' about your book to potential customers can be a labour intensive business if it is done manually. However, the process can be somewhat simplified if you can use the 'mail-merge' facilities on your WP. This involves creating a standard letter 'template' with blanks for names and addresses. A file of names and addresses, maintained separately, is 'merged' with this document in such a way that they are inserted in to the appropriate positions on the letter template. When a merge is performed, a separate letter is produced for each name and address. This technique is very common - for example, the personalised competition 'draws' you receive periodically through the post. You may like to build your own list of names and addresses for likely prospective customers, for example from a directory listing of companies or societies published in directories available in your local library. Alternatively, it is possible to purchase mailing lists. Various organisations will sell you their list of members and their addresses on 3.5" floppy disks. These can be used for merging into your standard letter.

By placing the address of your prospective customer in the appropriate place on a letter (usually near the top left-hand side), you can fold the page so that it shows through the clear panel of a windowed envelope. This saves time as it avoids the need to address the envelope separately.

To send an envelope second class mail with your flyer or brochure might cost you £0.35. That is almost 3 to the £1. For £350 you can send 1,000. This for example, would cover all the UK universities, colleges and more besides or many members of a club or association. It is worth a try. Identify your market and visit your local library for potential source lists.

8.5 Terms and conditions

Before you begin trading you should set out your terms and conditions. Look on the back of most order forms and you will find a comprehensive list of terms and conditions. If your publishing company grows to any size you may also need a comprehensive policy but for the fledgling enterprise something much simpler will do. Try and hold to the following basic terms and conditions:

- 📖 For private buyers, cheque with order.
- 📖 For companies and other institutions insist upon pre-payment by cheque or an official purchase order before you despatch a book with an invoice.
- 📖 The invoice states that payment is expected within a set number of days of receipt of goods (we state 15 days).
- 📖 If the book is not required it can be returned providing it is returned in the same condition it was sent. If the order was pre-paid a full refund will be given. (No quibbling here - it is not worth the hassle!)
- 📖 For Internet enquiries, we will normally accept an e-mail as an order and a book can be despatched with invoice. If payment is not received within a period of 4 weeks, send reminders by e-mail.

8.5.1 Discounts

Selling books in quantity direct to bookshop chains and distributors, will require price negotiations. You must expect to give substantial discounts on the normal cover price (40-55%). Selling in small numbers, however, is another matter. In the UK, you can give discounts at your discretion, but this is not always the case for other countries. In the USA, for example, you must maintain a consistent discounting policy or you could fall foul of fair competition rules and the Federal Trade Commission. The FTC requires you to offer the same pricing policy to all 'like' customers. Formulate a discounting policy that you think is appropriate; we generally offer the following terms:

Non-trade orders
- 📖 No discount on orders for single books.
- 📖 10% on 2-5 books
- 📖 Negotiable for greater numbers.

Trade orders (bookshops have to make a profit)
- 📖 Generally 15% on orders made via Tele-ordering

Concessions for Students, Unemployed and OAPs.
- 📖 At our discretion!

8.6 Processing Sales Orders

If you are unfamiliar with basic business methods and invoicing principles we strongly advise you to obtaining further reading material on the subjects of starting up a business, accounting, book keeping, etc. The financial control of your enterprise must be rigorous and ultimately open to scrutiny by accountants and or tax authorities. *(See Maintaining Sales Records in section 8.7)*

8.6.1 Setting up a bank account

Before you start to trade we recommend that you set up a separate bank account to handle the financial transactions for your publishing enterprise. This will enable you to keep the financial records separate and distinct from your personal or any other business affairs that you might have. Keep your records meticulously, recording both income from sales and outgoing expenses and drawings for income, etc.

8.6.2 Invoicing

One of the basic documents you will need is an invoice that is issued to customers regardless of whether orders are pre-paid or not. By this stage you should be quite familiar with using a DTP package and will probably have little difficulty in constructing a personalised invoice proforma. These may then be filled in by hand, or more conveniently, completed using your PC. If possible, use your DTP or spreadsheet to record customer order details and to produce an invoice. The most important details that are required for an invoice are as follows:

- The issuer of the invoice (i.e. you or your organisation).
- Your address, telephone no., fax no., e-mail address, telex, etc.
- A unique invoice number.
- The customer to whom the invoice is sent. Note that the address will not always be the same as the one to where the goods were sent.
- The invoice issue date - (tax point).
- Your customer's order no., if there was one.
- A description of the goods and the quantity
- Unit price, any discount and net price: (unit price less discount) multiplied by the quantity.
- Any additional postage and packing.
- Any tax (N.B. In the UK VAT is not currently charged on books).
- How and where the remittance should be sent.
- If overseas, the currency conversion to be used.
- PAID WITH THANKS if the order was pre-paid.

118

A Typical Invoice (for example purposes only)

Good Fortune Book Company
(GF Books)
INVOICE

The Dower House,
Little Compton,
Cwmbran,
Gwent
NP45 7RG
Great Britain

Tel/Fax +44 (0)1345 675234
e-mail   sales@gfbooks.co.uk

To: Mr John Daniels 2210 South Wells Road, Arlington, Virginia 22205 USA	
Invoice Number: 1126	
Date: 1ˢᵗ March 1997	
Your Order No: by e-mail	

Description of Goods	Qty	Unit Price	Cost
Book: "A Practical Guide to Making Parachutes" ISBN 0 65432 456 3	1	15.99	15.99
Excess Postage			3.00
Please make cheques payable to GF Books.	**TOTAL**		**£18.99***

Exchange rate used 29/7/97 : £1 = US$1.62   conversion = $30.76

Please make payment within 15 days. Basis is Sale or Return. Please return book(s) in good condition if not required. The invoice is made out in UK Pounds which is our preferred currency to minimise bank charges. However, payments by cheques / bank orders made out in local currency are acceptable at the prevailing exchange rate.

Bank Details:	Fist National Bank of Wales PLC. Cwmbran, Town Branch, 45 Corn Square, Cwmbran, New Town, Gwent NP99 1AB , UK
Sort Code:	99 21 13
Account Number:	11232104
Account Name:	GF Books

✂ -

Please return this slip with your remittance   Invoice No. 1126   £18.99

GF Books, The Dower House
Little Compton
Cwmbran, Gwent
NP45 7RG, UK

Mr John Daniels
2210 South Wells Road,
Arlington, Virginia 22205
USA

Payment method ✓
Cheque
BACS
Other

© Domanski & Irvine 1997

> **Tip:** Windowed envelopes: when creating an invoice proforma or letter, position the customer's name and address in such a position that, when the paper is folded, these details will be visible through the envelope window. This does away with the necessity of addressing envelopes separately saving a great deal of time and bother.

8.6.3 The Invoice Cycle

Despite a request for payment within 15 days of receipt of order on the bottom of our invoice, we have found that most invoices are paid within a period of 4-6 weeks. In practice, we do not send out reminders until 6 weeks have passed after despatch. In the UK, companies and other institutions have 'invoicing cycles' normally in the range 1 - 3 months. Reluctantly we have come to terms with this as a fact of life!

8.6.4 Book trade orders and TeleOrdering

Regrettably, members of the book trade are amongst the slowest of payers. We receive many orders from bookshops and book distributors via a trade TeleOrdering service. A printed order form arrives on behalf of a book shop or distributor and we duly despatch a book(s) to the appropriate address with an invoice cross-referenced to any order number. We then expect to have to wait for up to 4 months for payment if no reminder is sent! Three months until payment is about the norm for trade orders although some companies are swifter at paying than others. Note that when processing orders by way of the TeleOrdering service, be careful that your invoice is sent to the correct address. Very often, books have to be despatched to a book shop at one address and the invoice sent to an accounts department at another address (e.g. at Head Office at a different location.).

8.6.5 PO Box numbers and cheques

Where your orders and cheques are sent to, is a decision that needs careful consideration. Rather than have orders sent directly to your home address, you may prefer to use a Post Office Box Number to which correspondence is directed. A PO Box will cost you about £50 per year. For a few pounds more, you can arrange for the contents of your PO Box to be sent directly to your home address. This may save you an inconvenient trek down to the Post Office to collect any mail. Remember to check your PO Box regularly! Some journals and magazines require advertisers to forward goods to the customer within a set period (normally 7 days) if money is sent with an order. This will not give you much leeway to process and send the order if you check the PO Box only once a week. This period may be extended if a response is made to the customer in writing.

8.6.6 *Credit and charge card sales*

This is the most efficient and potentially profitable means of processing sales. Many, if not the majority of customers, now prefer to make their purchases by credit card. This method of selling is particularly easy for the customer who wants to order over the phone simply by quoting a card number. The vendor benefits from the spontaneity factor - the customer can order the book on a whim before there is a change of mind. You will attract impulse buyers: they see the advertisement, pick up the phone, quote name and number and expect dispatch the same or next day. A cheque sent by post, needs a letter, envelope, stamp, etc. and, if your customer intends to do this, perhaps after a hard days work, your potential order might be overlooked or forgotten! Credit card buyers also have enhanced consumer protection through the credit card rules. If you are selling direct, without credit card sales you could be losing out.

However, if you do want to accept credit cards, there is more work for you to do! You will need someone on the end of the phone or fax machine to take orders (the fax machine is particularly useful if you are selling across the world i.e. across time zones). Credit card customers will also expect their goods to be delivered within a day or so! You will need special equipment to process transactions for the leading credit card companies. This has to be arranged through the banks - and will involve a set-up charge. The credit card companies will also take a commission of 3.5 - 10%, depending on your turnover, but this should be negotiable. You may also be required to pay a monthly service fee. Your bank should be able to advise you on their credit card merchandising schemes. You could be in a Catch-22 situation; on the one hand, if you are selling direct and do not have credit card facilities you could lose sales. On the other hand, you will have to maintain a certain minimum number of sales per month to make the investment and commitment worthwhile.

An alternative to processing credit cards yourself, is to come to an arrangement with a local company to take the orders for you. They may even be willing to package and post your goods. This will be at a cost, however, and you will also be involved in arranging money transfers, etc. On your £15 book, you might be charged £2.50 - £3.50 per copy for just handling the credit card transaction. This might appear to be a large dent in your margin but it is still a considerably greater return than selling through normal retail outlets that would cost you 40-55% of the cover price.

Credit card details by e-mail

We have used an electronic credit card order entry form embedded in our web pages (web pages are covered in the next chapter). Many customers from abroad prefer to use this means of buying because of its convenience, although sending credit card details over the Internet is not without some risk. Many Internet providers can now provide 'secure' facilities for this kind of transaction. The customer fills in their details on their PC screen and the order form is converted into an e-mail. When it is received, the order can be processed and the book(s) despatched. Some customers who do not wish to send their details electronically over the Internet, print out the form, fill it out by hand and then fax it or send it by post. Note that, like receiving credit card orders over the telephone, orders by e-mail are regarded as 'unverified' as no signature is received nor is there contact with the customer in person. This carries slightly greater risk for the credit card companies - and you will be charged extra for this kind of transaction.

8.6.7 Overseas earnings (exports)

These are to be encouraged - primarily because you will be aiding your country's export effort and earning valuable foreign currency; you will also find it very satisfying selling your book abroad and communicating with people in far-flung places. That's the good news! However, you will soon realise why some exporters find selling goods for non-home currencies rather troublesome.

> Exporting your books can be very worthwhile BUT do consider any extra costs associated with processing overseas orders:
> - Banking charges
> - Currency exchange rates
> - Extra postage
>
> Processing charges on small transactions (such as for individual books) may eat into your margin to the extent that it is not profitable for you to export. You may need to add an extra service charge to your normal price to cover the additional expense. Find out from your bank, in advance, what the cheque processing costs are and whether cheques can be batched together. Charge extra postage where necessary.

Credit card transactions are relatively easy as the currency conversions are done for you automatically by the credit card companies and you can get a reasonable rate of exchange. [The same process, but in reverse, if you use your Visa or Mastercard, etc. on a foreign holiday]. Processing cheques is another matter. In the UK, if you present a cheque from a foreign bank in a foreign currency to be paid in to your account, you will be charged for it to be cashed. Charges vary from bank to bank but £5 is currently the average. The banks have to negotiate between themselves for exchange rates and transfers. Be warned, it can take up to a month for the cheque to clear and exchange rates do not always work in your favour. For a £15 book, a £5 processing charge is not economic! Note, however, that these charges can be minimised by batching cheques (of the same currency) as you will usually be charged the £5 for one cheque or ten when presented together. For example, with 5 cheques or more you will only be paying the equivalent of £1 or less per order - a significant improvement on £5 per cheque.

Customs declarations
In the UK, selling books to other EU countries does not require customs declarations. If you send your books to most other countries, including the USA, you will be required to complete and sign a declaration form (a small green sticker obtainable from the Post Office) and attach it to your packet. You need to specify contents, weight, value and whether it is merchandise or a gift.

8.7 Maintaining Sales Records and Book Keeping

We strongly advise the reader to acquire some knowledge of the fundamentals of starting and running a business: particularly looking after accounts and book-keeping. There are many publications covering all aspects of this subject and your local library, as ever, would be a good port of call to find something suitable. It is most important that you keep a record of all financial transactions connected with your publishing enterprise - expenses and revenue no matter what the scale of the operation. As has been mentioned previously, it is advisable to use a separate bank account to administer your book sales and expenses. In this way business is conducted separately from any personal banking arrangements. [You may, however, decide that a new account is unnecessary if you already have a separate one for business that can accommodate any book transactions to your existing business affairs.] At some point you will need to declare any earnings to the tax authorities and you will need to produce accounts for evidence of earnings, expenditure, withdrawals, etc.

Do give some thought to organising a 'system' for record keeping before business really gets underway so that this aspect of publishing is an orderly routine. If orders start to roll in, it is surprising how quickly you can get behind with maintaining the accounts. Use your PC to help you; there are a number of reasonably priced software packages available that can be used for recording accounts, and producing reports. If the level of business warrants it, money spent on such a package is well justified. For only a small level of sales activity, however, simple spreadsheets constructions - for recording income from sales and expenses will probably be all you require to keep control of the business. We have found that a spreadsheet containing the following information with automatic column totalling for numeric fields enables us to monitor income, origin of orders, late payers, sales volumes and other statistics. It is easy to create and simple to maintain.

Column	Example
Invoice number	1234
Customer order number (if applicable)	B123275/A
Customer name	JSmith-Ohio
Customer type (individual, bookshop, company, etc.)	COMP (Company)
Country	USA
Date of despatch/ invoice	12/3/97
Quantity	1
Value (£)	£17.99
Date invoice paid	5/4/97
Amount received	17.99
Currency paid in	US$
Extra postage charged to customer	£3.42
Actual postage	£5.31
Where seen (e.g. advert, bookshop or Internet)	WWW (web page)
Notes	"Urgent order"

8.8 Other Sources of Revenue and Funding

Funding

If you intend to work on your book full-time and need financial support then you might consider applying for assistance from one of a number of funding bodies. *The Writer's Handbook 1997* (published annually) is an invaluable book that lists many contact addresses including an extensive list of organisations that may be able to help you. Depending on the organisation, various criteria for eligibility such as experience, age, region and topic may be applied by different organisations who you may wish to approach for a grant, award or bursary.

Prizes

You will undoubtedly have heard of the Booker and Whitbread prizes for literature in the UK but you may be surprised at the number of other prizes that are awarded each year. Some prize-giving organisations do not require you to enter your work directly, rather, they rely on nominations from a committee. Others, however, invite authors to submit their work for competitive entry. Again, refer to *The Writer's Handbook* for a comprehensive list of competitions and prizes.

Public Lending Rights

An advantage of selling to libraries (in the UK) is the additional income that arises from the Public Lending Rights scheme (PLR). In effect, authors receive a small fee each time a book is borrowed from a public library. Currently, the fee earned by each 'borrowing' is approximately 2p. The maximum fee that may be earned is at present set at £6,000 per annum but this sum is attained by only a handful of very popular authors (less than 100 in 1996). To reach the maximum, your book would have to be borrowed a staggering 300,000 times. If your book was only borrowed 1000 times around the country, the PLR would earn you the princely sum of £20 so it is advisable not to order the yacht on the basis of your PLR, earnings! Whilst not a great sum, your earnings from this means should be regarded as a bonus. The PLR scheme, additionally, does give the author some idea of the level of interest that a book has generated. To benefit from the PLR you will need to obtain an application form giving details of yourself as author and a list of your publications to be included in the scheme. Payments to authors are made in February and, to be eligible for any possible payment, applications should be received before the end of May the previous year. The address you should write to for a PLR application form is:

The Public Lending Right Office,
Bayheath House,
Prince Regent Street,
Stockton-on-Tees,
Cleveland
TS18 1DF (Tel. 01642 604699)

8.8.1 Spin-Offs

Publishing your book is one thing, profiting from it is another. However, book sales need not be the only source of income derived from your endeavours. You may also be able to profit indirectly as a consequence of being a published author: 'Spin-offs' are products and services that can be marketed as a result of your book. If you had a number one best-seller, careful marketing might lead to a lucrative deal for film or television rights. These in turn could lead to other 'merchandise' - tee-shirts, toys, mementoes and a host of other paraphernalia. ...Coming back down to earth, however, how can you, as a one-person enterprise, most likely benefit from spin-offs from say, a technical or 'How to' title?

There are number of options which are worthwhile exploring. They broadly fall into two categories:

- As an author, you can develop and capitalise on your new-found 'expert' or celebrity status.
- You may be able to market derivatives based upon the subject matter of your book.

Capitalising on your status as an author/ expert

Society in general respects its authors; you may even find that, locally at least, you have become a minor celebrity, one of the Intelligentsia! Those who have made their mark in technical, managerial, academic and other non-fiction categories usually find that they have enhanced career prospects merely by being marked out as people who have risen above the norm. Details of your publication should definitely be displayed prominently on your c.v. You will find, at the very least, that your book will become a talking point at job interviews and give you a territory upon which to expound with gusto and authority. Additionally, there are other ways that your expert status can be exploited. For example:

📖 *Lecturing*: Enhance your earnings on the basis that your book labels you an expert. People may pay to come and hear you talk or alternatively, organisations may pay you to go and address them at their premises. Many companies often invite lecturers and trainers to give talks and courses in-house rather than pay for expensive and/ or less convenient off-site courses. There are any number of organisations that use guest speakers and lecturers.

📖 *Consultancy*: Like lecturing, you may be in demand for your consultancy services. Your advice is sought in your specialist area and you may be paid handsomely for it. Many organisations, government and commercial, rely on outside consultants on short term (a few days) or medium term contracts (years) to fill the gaps in their in-house knowledge and skills. Aim for short well paid assignments or longer term retainers. If you would like to pursue this route but are unsure how to proceed, or, even whether there is a market for your services and expertise, you may find there are specialist agencies available to match client and consultant Skills in the fields of computing, engineering and management are particularly in demand and are well served by a large number of agencies who match skills to clients' requirements.

📖 *Journalism*: Again your expertise may enable you to pursue paid work writing articles or features in journals or magazines. There may be an opportunity to plug your book(s) or review those of other authors. Being in the press does enhance your status as an expert and can be invaluable in selling more books by the publicity that you can generate. *The Writer's Handbook* provides an extensive list of journals and magazines that commission work; it also details the rates of payment to contributors.

Derivatives from your book(s)
Having written your book, you may have ideas about re-using information, themes or ideas in alternative products. Of course the scope in this area depends very much on the type of book you have written. Here are just a few ideas:

📖 *Plays, radio, television and film adaptations* of your book - if you are lucky! Be adventurous: write to editors, commissioning producers, etc. Just as for journalists you need a lucky break, just one piece of work such as a short story for radio to get the ball rolling. Yet again *The Writer's Handbook* is an invaluable source of contacts.

📖 *Electronic publications*: We have deliberately avoided this subject in this book as it is very specialised and still in its infancy. However, slowly but surely, the electronic media are gaining in popularity and the opportunities for using it are growing. In particular, if you are publishing data or data-rich information which readers may wish to "copy and paste" into their own computer documents, then consider publishing a separate CD-ROM format edition of your book. CD-ROMs are cheap to produce and take up little storage space. You may find that the margin of profit on a CD-ROM edition is considerably higher than that for a conventionally produced book. Electronic publications available for downloading from the Internet are also gaining popularity BUT getting people to part money for downloaded files is still difficult. It is often better to make available just selected sections of your work for downloading as a 'taster' in the hope that readers will want to buy the actual book. No doubt the 'paperless' society will be with us one day...... but not just yet.

📖 *Pamphlets and smaller booklets*: You may be able to produce condensed versions such as 'pocket guides', planners, training manuals workshop manuals, recipe cards, fact sheets etc.

📖 *'Kits'*: These are packs, perhaps containing your book or a derivative of it, together with training material, software or other samples, etc. You might also consider making a video (e.g. for training purposes) to include in a kit. Prices for kits can be much higher than the original price of your book.

📖 *Children's books* can lead to a number of spin-offs: toys, magazines, educational material, printed fabrics, etc. The appeal of your book and your shrewdness as a marketeer come to prominence here.

9.   Using The Internet

9.1 What is it?

The Internet has its origins in the US military. It started life as ARPANET and was designed to be a resilient wire based communication network comprising thousands of discrete computers inter-connected by telephone lines. It was perceived as being indestructible - unless all its components were eliminated.

Other uses of such an effective communications system were soon realised and it became a boon to scientific and academic institutions as it grew into a world wide network. Since every computer connected to it has a unique address, it provides a remarkably efficient means of message and data communication between institutions. Individual 'mailboxes' can be allocated at each point and so any person with an e-mail (electronic mail) address can exchange messages with any other e-mail address.

9.2 How Can it be Useful to a Publisher?

For three very good reasons:

- World-wide access for potential customers to your 'virtual shop'.
- World-wide communication by electronic mail (e-mail).
- Information and data gathering on a vast scale.

9.2.1 The World Wide Web (WWW)

At the time of writing, there are an estimated 40 million+ users of the Internet or 'Information Superhighway' as it is sometimes known. Present projections suggest that there will be over 100 million users by the end of the decade. The actual number of people connecting to it may be underestimated as this figure includes multiple users - institutional accounts for companies, colleges, government departments and other organisations. Until the beginning of 1994, the Internet's main use was for the transmission of data, messages by e-mail,

Newsgroups, etc. However, since then, the invention of the World Wide Web (WWW) has caused a revolution in electronic communication as the Internet has become a wonderfully effective service for disseminating formatted text and images.

Web pages can be designed to look like pages of a book, advertisements, booking forms, credit card slips and all manner of documents. They can incorporate a host of other useful features and be viewed by virtually all Internet account holders who may be situated anywhere in the world. During 1994 and 1995 the number off accessible pages grew at the phenomenal rate of approximately 10-15% per month. At the beginning of 1995 there were just over 4.5 million accessible web pages. By the end of 1995 there were 10 million and at the time of completion of this book (June 1997), Alta Vista, the premier Internet 'search engine', had well over 30 million accessible pages registered in its database.

Web page owners include private individuals, consultancies, companies, governments and other institutions such as schools, colleges and museums, newspapers and magazines. This new medium for displaying text and images is a significant development in global communication and is rapidly becoming the predominant method for global marketing and information dissemination. If you doubt this, you have not seen it in action. For once you can believe the press hype, it is not fiction!

Access to the WWW is achieved by way of user-friendly software on an office or home based PC, but there are developments afoot to introduce cheap 'smart' telephone systems. These appliances, equipped with a small screen, will not require the need for such expensive and highly specified computer equipment and will offer users the facility to view web information, collect and send electronic mail. Television companies are also experimenting with incorporating web text and images into teletext-type systems. In the longer term, therefore, it is anticipated that access to the WWW will be even more widespread than it is at present and essential for businesses, educational institutions and governments to be represented on it.

What is so compelling about pages on the WWW is that there is no distinction between local, national or international access to them; there are no boundaries. Information put on a web page from our base in Leominster, Herefordshire, is just as accessible in Hereford (12 miles distant), London, Los Angeles in the USA or Sydney in Australia. To create and maintain a web page for marketing purposes is remarkably inexpensive compared with advertising in the traditional media. A web page on the Internet can cost you less for one whole year than single (one-off) small insertion in your local newspaper and remember this is global as opposed to local coverage! Although much information you have to offer may only be appropriate to a local market, usage of the Internet is growing rapidly. The time when users will find it just as useful to look up local and national information on the Internet as traditional sources, is probably not far off. Already, tourist information, health facilities, local government, local businesses are available on web pages and it is anticipated that this trend will continue.

> Since first advertising on the Internet with our own web pages in mid-1995, we have sold copies of our first book on relational database design to over 20 countries. We have not placed a single advertisement in any other media outside the UK.

Many thousands of individuals and organisations around the world have already realised the potential advantage to them of advertising and marketing on the Internet. Publishers and book shops are no exception and it is possible to view book titles in 'virtual bookshops' and order them from the comfort and convenience of your office or home (or wherever the PC is located). Web pages have the additional advantage of enabling visitors to contact the page owners directly via e-mail so dialogue can be conducted between potential customer and the publisher. This feature truly provides a very inexpensive and easy means of global communication.

> E-mail via the Internet has distinct advantages over conventional mailing methods. 1) It is *cheaper*, you will pay a set connection fee per month to an Internet Provider, typically £7.50 - £12 per month. Your only other expense for e-mail will be locally-rated telephone charges while connected to your Internet service (if you are on cable, this may be free). 2) *Speed*, your mail can be delivered in as little time as a few minutes to most places around the world. 3) You can send the same message to *multiple addresses*. 4) All your correspondence is conveniently *recorded* on your PC in 'in' and 'out' mail boxes on your PC and can be viewed at any time (offline).

9.2.2 Web Browsers

To access and display web pages you will need a 'Web Browser' program on your PC. A web page is accessed by entering its unique address or 'URL' (Universal Resource Locator). When connected to the Internet, the browser will connect to the computer on which the page resides (the web site). The route by which contact is made may be long and complicated, perhaps across oceans and continents and via satellites but contact is normally made in just a few seconds. The contents of the web page will automatically start 'downloading' through the telephone network to your PC and, unless you specify otherwise, text and images will be displayed upon your PC screen. The rate at which this occurs is normally limited by the speed at which your modem can transmit and receive data. Images take the longest time to complete as they require large amounts of data to be transmitted. This is where your modem speed is significant as, the faster it can work, the quicker the text and images will appear on your browser and the lower your telephone charges will be. A 28,800bps modem is preferable, 14,400 bps is usually satisfactory but anything less is too slow to use the web effectively (although probably quite adequate for e-mail and other text based Internet services).

Below is a reproduction of a web page viewed using the Microsoft Explorer browser, one of the leading packages.

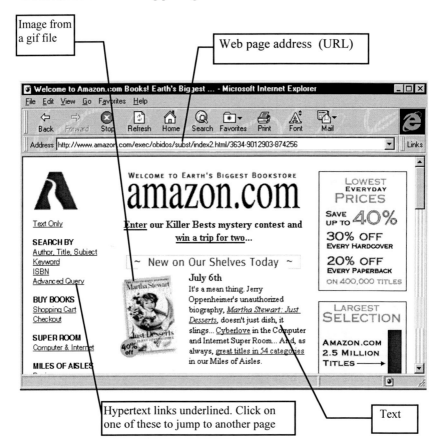

Image from a gif file

Web page address (URL)

Hypertext links underlined. Click on one of these to jump to another page

Text

'Surfing the Net'

Net 'surfing' is rather an over-statement. In the context of the WWW, it involves connecting to one web page and then clicking on a 'hypertext link' that will conduct you to another web page. Hypertext links are normally distinguished from other text by being displayed in a different colour. They may also be represented by a labelled symbol or stylised graphic. Whatever its appearance, attached to the label is the URL of the web page it represents. When you click on it with your mouse, the browser initiates a connection to it and, if it is located, the current page on your screen is replaced with the new one. By selecting hyperlinks in succession you could be traversing communications links around the globe - hence the expression 'net surfing'! The browser enables you to save the URLs of your 'favourite' web pages and by retaining backward and forward pointers, it allows you to go back and forth to pages you have already visited. Redisplay of pages you have already visited is much quicker as the information is retained on your PC.

9.3 What you need to access the Internet

Quite simply, a PC, a modem, a telephone socket, Internet account and some additional Internet software.

9.3.1 Internet Service Providers and Internet

The Internet is a vast network of computer to computer on-line connections. However, unless you are a major company or institution (and have a significant communications budget), your own PC will not need to be on-line continuously. Instead, you only connect to the Internet as and when you need to, through an account supplied by a 'Service Provider'. Providers *are* on-line all the time and will facilitate your gateway onto the network. Your provider will set you up a mailbox with your own e-mail address and, should you want them, allocate you disk space for your own web pages - your web site. When you have an account you will be given a telephone number(s) for your PC to dial into via the modem. At the other end of the line will be the provider's modem that will route you into the Internet. Most commercial providers now supply national coverage with local-rated telephone numbers. Thus you will be able to access sites anywhere in the world and all you will be charged is a fixed monthly connection fee plus the cost of the local call. If you have a cable telephone service you may not even be paying for your local calls!

9.3.2 E-mail

Your e-mail address will be a unique name and address to which other people can direct mail (electronic messages) to you over the Internet. It will also be the signature of any mail that you send to others. Your service provider will allocate you with one (or more) e-mail addresses which usually take the form:

myname@account.provider.domain

where *provider.domain* is the name and extension of your provider . *account* is the name of the account that you are allocated (e.g. your company name) and *myname* will be a personalised component of the name.

For example, if you were to use our own providers (u-net of Warrington) you might have an address such as:

joebloggs@xyzco.u-net.com

At extra cost, your e-mail address may be further personalised, e.g joebloggs@xyzco.com This, however, requires further international registration and an annual maintenance fee.

Domains: These are extensions which signify the provider's type of organisation, e.g. '.com' in the example means 'commercial'. Other types include: .gov (government), .edu (universities), .net (network resources). Further extensions may be used, e.g. country codes: . uk

---

Your service provider will furnish you with the software needed to use e-mail, browse the WWW and other services available on the Internet. We will not discuss this extensively but suffice it to say that there is plenty of software available for use with the Internet. Much of it is in the 'Public Domain' and available free. More fully featured software can be bought. Note that the latest web browsers, e.g. Netscape's Navigator and Microsoft's Explorer also incorporate e-mail facilities.

9.4 Creating your own Web Pages

Web pages comprise the following primary components as illustrated in the previous example:

📖 Text	Your message
📖 Images	Pictures
📖 Hypertext links	Jump points to link to other pages

All web sites have what is termed a 'Home Page'. This is the 'head' page, and a springboard where the owner declares who and what they are, and in what they are specialised or interested. Commercially oriented sites should incorporate an eye-catching image or logo. There are so many pages to visit and an interesting picture will catch the attention and hopefully be remembered - just like any other form of advertising.

9.4.1 The Home Page

The top of the home page usually contains a welcoming introduction, below this could be further text and images. For example, a manufacturing company might publish a general statement about its product range. Thereafter, there could be a number of highlighted text areas or thumbnail size images that are hypertext links leading to other pages with more specific information. If products are being advertised, these other pages on the 'web site' may contain images, descriptions and specifications. The visitor is directed to jump from page to page, guided by hypertext links.

As an example, imagine a publisher specialising in gardening and botanical books, he might organise his home pages to look something like this:

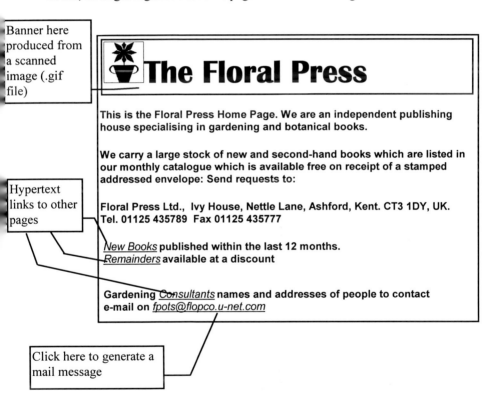

It starts with an announcement of who the owner is, what they are and where they are located. Further information can be obtained by selecting, i.e. pointing the mouse cursor and clicking, on the hypertext links that are underlined in the diagram (they are normally blue and underlined). For example, if a user clicked on *New Books* another page would appear:

134

 # Floral Press New Books

We are pleased to offer the following new books published by Floral Press:

Click on underlined titles for further details.

"A History of the Rose" by Florence Bunda 1995, 212pp 105 photos and illustrations. The history of the cultivation of the rose family from the ancient Egyptians to the present day. £17.99

"Wheelbarrow Maintenance" by Arthur Wheeler 1994, 176pp 34 photos. Everything you could possibly want to know about your wheelbarrow. £7.95

"Bedding Plants And Other Perversions" by Harry Clogmore 1994, 321pp 130 illustrations and photos. A look under the cloche. £18.49

For details on how to order from Floral Press see *Order Details*
Note that we welcome personal callers 7 days a week!
Return to Floral Press *Home page*

This second page not only contains a list of new books but has further links to give greater levels of detail. Note also the link provided at the bottom of the page to provide easy navigation back to the home page.

The virtual catalogue
As mentioned earlier, both text and images (and sound and movie clips if you really want them!) can be displayed. The banners on the pages illustrated, are displayed from image files held along with the text. They would have been scanned in by the page compiler as described earlier. The use of images can be much more extensive. You could put together a 'virtual' catalogue, displaying your wares as images. You then have the flexibility to rearrange or change your catalogue at will. If users so desire, they can obtain 'hard copy' of your web page(s) on a printer. As you can imagine, this kind of set-up does give you considerable scope for design and flair to create your 'shop front' to the world.

9.4.2 How are web pages created
Web pages use a formatting language called HTML (HyperText Markup Language). In its unconverted form (source), it looks rather strange but a web browser program interprets it and displays it as a formatted document. To compile a web page it is helpful to understand the basics of HTML so that you can manipulate it. In reality this is no problem because you can use a basic template or model yours on somebody else's HTML text. For example, here is a part of our home page in the HTML language:

```
<!-- Document type HTML-->
<HTML>
<img src="motif2.gif" align=center>
<HEAD><TITLE>Welcome    to    the    Domanski-Irvine    Book    Company    Home
Page</TITLE></HEAD>
<P>
<BODY>
<h4><I>Introducing:</I></H4>
<H1> A Practical Guide to Relational Database Design </H1> <hr><P>
<I> by Peter Domanski & Philip Irvine </I>
<P>
                    Ref 1236,
                    Cwmbran,
                    Gwent,
                    NP44 5YH,
                    United Kingdom
Remember to state your name and address clearly with your order!
</PRE>
<P>
<ADDRESS>For further  information contact
<A HREF="mailto:info@dibookco.u-net.com">
info@dibookco.u-net.com
</A>
</ADDRESS>
<HR>
<P>
This page was last updated 1/8/96
<P>
</BODY>
</HTML>
```

Very few people now create their web pages by writing directly in HTML. Web
page composition is now mostly done using web page authoring tools. There are
presently many such tools to choose from and as this topic is relatively new, it is
a very active and lucrative area for software companies to produce products.
Amongst the pre-eminent products, Microsoft Publisher '97 has an excellent web
page composition facility incorporating helpful 'wizards' and pre-configured
formats. Microsoft Word '97 also lets you turn an ordinary document into a web
page so the user should have little difficulty in mastering the art. Creating your
pages is now a comparatively simple process - but you do need to use your
creative flair to create interesting and effective pages - i.e. your international
shop front!

To create individual web pages or pages for an entire 'web site', you create pages either manually in HTML, or using an authoring tool saving them in files on your PC. All testing and composition is done locally (i.e. off-line) and your pages can be viewed directly using your web browser. When you are satisfied with the results, the web pages, held in files on your PC need to be copied to a directory on the web server computer. Space for web pages will have been allocated to you by your Internet Provider (with whom you have an account). Transfer is achieved using a utility (FTP - File Transfer Protocol). When the pages have been 'uploaded' they can be viewed from across the Internet. New pages and changes to your existing pages are thereafter created on your PC and uploaded to the web server as before. This process can be done at any time so you can change your pages at will. *If you are not confident about designing and creating web pages yourself, there are a growing number of agencies willing to perform this service for you.*

9.5 Advantages of Using the Internet and Web Pages

To market a book, other product or service, effective advertising is crucial. However, it must now be apparent to the reader that advertising in the traditional media of specialist journals and the press can be prohibitively expensive. This is especially so for a small organisation such as a fledgling publishing company. There are two conflicting factors: the need to reach as many people as possible and the need to commit the minimum outlay to secure this goal. The WWW can achieve this as, by creating web pages you can represent your products in greater depth. If you cannot sell sufficient numbers of books on the Internet alone, you need only place strategic and succinct advertisements in journals drawing attention to your WWW address (see 8.4.4). Anyone with access to the Internet (40million +) can visit your pages at leisure. They will be able to get a comprehensive view of your book (Introduction, TOC, information about the authors, etc). Importantly, the web page will also provide a means of automatic e-mail for enquiries and ordering. The information available by this method is far more extensive than you could possibly have provided with conventional advertisements.

There are, 'virtual bookshops' which can be viewed by those who know where to look, but by combining conventional advertising with substantial additional information on the Internet, you can have the following advantages:

1. Significantly reduce advertising costs by using smaller, strategically placed advertisements (which may also attract customers who do not use the Internet).
2. Increase the volume, quality and flexibility of information that can be made available (like browsing through a book in a bookshop - only

directed and structured). The information, built up of 'hypertext' links includes text, images (and now even sound and moving images).

3. You can change the composition of web pages on demand.

4. If selling by mail-order, a customer who has visited a web page will have a better idea of what he/she will be buying than an ordinary advertisement. This should lead to greater customer satisfaction.

5. Using e-mail links it provides a fast, easy and inexpensive communication channel for customer orders and enquiries.

6. There is no need for separate Home and Export advertising as there is no such distinction amongst the Internet 'community'. This can only be good for exports from the UK.

7. You can monitor the number of visits paid to your www page, hence gauge the interest generated.

8. You can link to other items which may be of interest to potential customers (hypertext links). Other www pages can also point to us (co-operatives in the making?)

9. You can provide free information to visitors thereby making yours a 'resource site', and by so doing, increasing interest in your site.

10. It can cost very little to set up and maintain! (for as little as £100 + VAT per annum excluding telephone connection charges.)

9.5.1 Advantages to the community and Small Businesses

Based in rural Herefordshire, our company, D-I Books, is an idyllic location in which to work but it is remote from traditional support services. Now, however, as far as communications are concerned, we are no longer disadvantaged by region or location. We, too, can reach and export around the world - the same as any of the other millions of Internet users whether based in major cities or in remote rural areas.

9.6 Getting Noticed on the WWW

At the beginning of this chapter we highlighted three main reasons for using the Internet. This is the third - Information gathering. There are organisations that make it their business to read all the accessible pages on the WWW and store all the keyword elements on massive databases. These databases facilitate 'search engines' which rely on extract information. Keyword searches are one of the main methods by which your web pages are found by other Internet users.

9.6.1 Using "Search Engines"

Internet users wanting to find specific information, about virtually any information under the sun, use their web browser to visit their favourite search 'engine' web site. Returning to our imaginary web pages for the Floral Press, the words 'Wheelbarrow' and 'Harry Clogmore' appear on one of the pages illustrated. If these pages were live on the WWW they would be recorded in the major Internet search engine databases such as 'Lycos' and 'Alta Vista'(both free services, see in the Appendix for their URLs). A search is initiated by entering one or more words into a keyword search box and within a few seconds the results of the search (currently through 30 million + pages) will be returned. If we had entered the words 'wheelbarrow' or 'clogmore', a brief abstract of the appropriate Floral Press web pages will be retrieved in the search results. (Maybe amongst thousands of other references if the search words were very common.) The extracts will contain hypertext URLs that can be selected in the normal way to access the particular pages of interest.

We discussed earlier the importance of a good title because of the increasing use of electronic keyword searches. This holds true for searches on the Internet. We receive a number of orders for our database book from people who have entered keyword sequences such as 'database' and 'design'. This results in our page being retrieved containing our title "A Practical Guide to Relational Database Design". However, unlike bibliographic searches performed using library software which key on title and abstracts keywords, the WWW search engines use all the words in web page text. You can use this knowledge to your advantage when designing your own web pages.

Whereas book titles need to be relatively short and succinct, there is no restriction to what text you use on a web page. You should, therefore, weave into the text all the words you can imagine that someone interested in your subject might enter in a keyword search: technical expressions, jargon and all - anything that draws attention to your web site. Of course you should be reasonable about this, your message should be clear and well considered, not an incomprehensible jumble of keywords. Just as you will be able to take advantage of search engines drawing attention to your web site, you will undoubtedly find Alta Vista and other tools invaluable for locating information that you require. As authors, we find the encyclopaedic facilities of the WWW incredibly useful in locating facts, services, organisations, individuals, data and all manner of material of interest to us. The WWW is *the* place to look first!

9.6.2 *Other ways of getting noticed on the WWW*

Although search engine databases are periodically updated by rescanning the WWW for new and changes to web pages, you can take additional steps to maximise your presence on the WWW. The Internet is well provided with specialist directories and listing agencies, many of which make no charge for adding your URL(s) to their own sites. The most prominent ones are Yahoo and Yellow Pages. These organisations organise their information by topic and sub-topic down several layers. These frequently visited services make their money largely by selling advertising space. To add your pages to their list you need to connect to their sites and fill in their electronic application forms. Other agencies, such as Postmaster charge for forwarding your information to a large number of other web sites, reviewers, news agencies, etc. They do, however, charge for this service (typically US $250 per web site) which you may find a worthwhile investment in the long term.

Another approach is to register your book(s) with on-line book shops which are growing in number. For an excellent example, see the www address for the Internet Bookshop given in the Appendix. They allow you to add comments to your own book entries as well as help you with on-line book promotions.

9.7 Last Words

We have not given instructions in the minutiae of DTP techniques or go into too great a depth in some of the many areas of publishing and marketing where there is much more detailed information available elsewhere. However, we have introduced the reader to all the major topics and processes that must be considered when planning and executing a publishing venture. We hope that the advice and shared experiences will be useful and demonstrate that it can and has been done successfully. The options and facilities available to an independent publisher have never been so great as at present. Consequently, for the first time we can say that the success of an enterprise ultimately depends upon imagination, skill and determination rather than substantial financial wherewithal and inside knowledge of the publishing industry. The brave new world of the Internet facilitating easily accessible, global communications from the home or office, has opened up possibilities for the sale and marketing of your books on all scales: local, national and international. The ease with which this can be done was unimaginable even five years ago. If you find the whole prospect too daunting, don't be overwhelmed as you will not require all of the skills at once - you will pick them up as you need them. Rome was not built in a day and neither can you become a successful publisher overnight. As we have ourselves found, if you have produced a book of wide appeal and genuine value, there is absolutely no reason why you should not succeed.

Good Luck!

Glossary

A3 Standard paper size 594 x 297mm (twice the size of A4).
A4 Standard paper size 210 x 297mm (exactly half A3).
A5 Standard paper size 148 x 210mm (exactly half A4).
Acknowledgements Thanks for help with preparation or contribution of material. Also crediting of trademarks or copyright.
AIDA Marketing term: Attention - Interest - Desire - Action
Appendix Section included at the back usually containing resources and reference material.
Alignment Setting the text so it begins and /or ends flush with the margin (*see justification*).
Barcode Sequence of vertical lines constituting a machine readable code. ISBN is held in the EAN 13 standard and displayed on the back cover.
Bibliography Section, usually at the back detailing full references of other work used and other reading matter.
Binding The method by which pages of a book are held together and attached to its cover, e.g. perfect binding.
Blurb Advertising matter, usually in the form of a 'flyer' or brochure.
Bitmap Electronic representation of an image. Diagrams and photographs can take longer to print than just text as a bitmap has to be downloaded to the printer.
Booklet Printing A method by which documents are printed on sheets of paper so that the sequence of pages allows you fold them into a booklet (and staple them in the middle pages).
Bps Bits per second. The rate of message send and receive achieved by a modem.
Bullet Points Small black circles or squares, usually indented to highlight a list (of points).
Case: Upper case (uc) capital letters, Lower case (lc) small letters.
CDROM Compact disk Read-Only Memory (but note that CD writing machines are available).
Check-digit An extra digit added to the end of a string of digits calculated in such a way so that the sum of the individual digits always has a predictable property - e.g. exactly divisible by 10. This helps to confirm that the the digits have been read correctly. This is important for a device such as a barcode scanner.
CIP Cataloguing In Publication: Scheme run by the British Library listing and summarising books before publication.
Clip Art Small, stylised diagrams used to highlight text or improve presentation.
Copyright The exclusive right of an author or illustrator or photographer to publish their own original work.
Copyright Page Declaration of copyright ownership. The copyright notice must include the word "copyright" and use the © symbol.

CPU Central Processing Unit, e.g. Pentium or 486. It is the PC's main processing unit.

Cut and Paste An editing technique that allows you to select text with a mouse, cut it out of its current position, click on the position where you would like it moved to and insert it with another click of the mouse (*see also 'drag and drop'*).

Database Formalised repository of data. Allows structured deposition and retrieval of data.

Dedication Someone nominated as being your inspiration, usually a loved one.

Despair A state of mind induced when a customer spots an obvious error in the text of your book.

Direct Sales Sales made direct to the customer, either by way of mail order advertising or the Internet. This method maximises your profit as no middlemen are involved and no discount need to be given.

Digital Camera New type of camera that records the image on a magnetic disk rather than film. Images at 600x600dpi or better can be transferred direct to the PC. Now a very viable alternative to scanning photographs taken with conventional cameras.

Dpi Dots per inch. A measurement of the resolution achieved by printers and an estimation of the definition achieved by a scanner.

Drag and Drop An editing technique that allows you to select text with a mouse, hold the mouse button down and 'drag' to a new position. When the mouse button is released, the text will be repositioned to the current cursor position (*see also 'cut and paste'*).

DTP Desk Top Publishing. Computer-based package used to write and format documents of publication standard. Combines text with images.

Duplex Printer A (laser) printer capable of printing on both sides of the paper without intervention.

Edition The version of a book. Although substantially the same, Subsequent editions will differ in content. The First Edition..... is the first time it is published.

Electronic Publishing. Publishing by means other than on paper. CDRom, web sites, document file. Difficult to make money at for the present. Most people still prefer to read books rather from a computer screen - despite   multi-media.

E-mail Electronically transmitted mail. Your Internet account will provide you with at least one mailbox to and from which mail is sent.

E-mail Address of the form myname@mycompany.provider.com, to which your mail is sent from and collected.

EPS File Encapsulated PostScript. A print file written using PostScript can be transferred to any other PostScript device. Hence you may be able to use a professional 1200dpi printer even though you developed your manuscript using a much cheaper 300dpi device.

Font The name of the typeface, e.g. Times Roman, Arial, Courier.

Font Size The size of the font is measured in 'points'. There are 72 points to the inch. This text size is 10pt.

Foreword An introduction by someone other than the author, usually a famous person or acknowledged authority.

Format The size shape, types of headings, text per page and other general construction factors.

Grey Scale Greys, or 'half-tones' are created by stippling, i.e. small dots of varying density according to shade. Note that this does not always photocopy very well.

Gsm Grams per square metre. Defines the weight of paper. Most books use 80-100gsm for the printed matter. Paperback covers are normally in the range 300-400gsm.

Gutter The inside margins of pages, closest to the spine.

Hardware Physical pieces of equipment: PC, printer, scanner, etc.

Headers Text appearing at the top of the page describing the contents below it. 'Running Heads' will change from page to page as topics change.

Icons Little symbols in a software package screen upon which to click to evoke a specific action, e.g. to cut text, you can select it with the mouse and select the scissors icon ✂.

Imprint The publishers' details at the beginning of the book.

Indenting Extra distance from a margin before the start of a line of text.

Inkjet (and **bubblejet**) **Printer** Printer that writes using rapid and directed burst of ink spray on to paper.

Internet Uncentralised world-wide network of linked computers through, and to which, communications are made using standardised protocols.

Internet Provider Company who rents access and space (for e-mail and web pages). Will provide you with your Internet account.

ISBN International Standard Book Number. The ISBN is a unique 10 digit number given to your book that will identify the country of registration, publisher and title of your book. Must be printed at the bottom of the back cover.

ISSN International Standard Serial Number used to identify a publication in successive parts. Contains a serial component for indefinite continuation. Used for magazines, periodicals, yearbooks, etc.

Italic Text of the same font that has been slanted to the right - like this - *useful for emphasis, notes and asides*.

Jubilation The feeling created when you receive your first paying order.

Justification Alignment of the edge of text, e.g. Left justified: left hand edge flush with left margin, right-hand edge is 'ragged'. Justified: both edges flush with margins.

Lamination A plastic based glossy coat given to a cover to make it more durable.

Layout The characteristics of margins, headings, spacing, columns, etc.

LCCN US Library of Congress Card Number. Number assigned to a book for identification purposes in US libraries - important if you want to sell to US libraries (N.B. over 100,000!).

Limp Trade term for a soft cover or paperback.

Manuscript Here, meaning a completed document in electronic format - will become your publication when printed.

Milestone A planning term: a significant event on a work plan, e.g. 'Publication date'.

Modem Modulator/ Demodulator. Device for communicating with other computers across the telephone network. Required for use with the Internet.

Net Book Agreement Defunct arrangement whereby British retailers would only sell books at the recommended retail price.

News Group A location on the Internet where correspondence is conducted in special interests. There are many 1000s of them. You can subscribe and contribute to News Groups. There are two types: moderated in correspondence is conducted through an editor or non-moderated that are a 'free for all' there being no central clearing house for contents.

N-up Printing Method by which multiple pages can be printed on a single sheet of paper. Supported by more sophisticated DTP packages and printers..

OCR Optical Character Recognition. Software often bundled free with a scanner can be used to read typed text on a page and create a text file to imported into a DTP document.

Off-set litho Modern printing press. A master 'plate' is created photographically. In the press itself, the inked plate image, mounted on a roller, is first transferred, or offset to a rubber 'blanket' on another roller and in turn this is applied to the paper. In this way the original plate is protected from the abrasive wear of the paper. These presses can produce many thousands of printed sheets per hour.

Page Orientation: Landscape - wider than it is tall. Portrait -taller than it is wide (normal for books).

Parallel Port Communications port on the back of the PC base unit used for a printer, external tape back-up or disk drive. May also be used by some types of scanner.

PC Personal Computer. Originates from the IBM PC - which started it all off.

PCL Printer Control language: protocol used by the majority of printers. Each type of printer has its own particular 'driver'. A document set-up to print on a particular make of printer is unlikely to print accurately on another type.

Photo-typesetting Method by which the print process can be effected by taking a photographic image of the pages to be printed.

Plug and Play Technique available for Windows 95 by which a hardware peripheral device (CD Rom, disk drive, etc.) can be installed and the software auto-detects and configures it without further intervention.

Point size Text character sizes are specified by point size. 1 point equals 1/72".

PostScript A printer control language. A document set-up to print on one particular PostScript printer, should be printable on any other device that supports PostScript. See EPS file.

PPI Pages Per Inch - a measure of paper bulk.

PPM Lasers and other types of printers are rated by pages per minute (ppm). The faster the better but a manufacturer's quoted speed is for optimum conditions - e.g. repeat printing of the same page. If there are images to print, transfer to the printer will be comparatively slow and the ppm will be nothing like the quoted ppm.

Preface A short personal introduction by the author. Explains aims, motivation and philosophy.

144

Prelims Pages at the start of the book preceding the TOC or Introduction Includes the half-title and title pages, copyright page, etc..

Print Run The number of copies produced in a batch of printing.

Public Domain Material that can be published free of copyright restrictions. Also refers to software that can be used without any licensing restrictions.

Ragged The effect of the edge of a paragraph where the text is not aligned flush with the margin.

RAM Random Access Memory 'Dynamic' memory used by your PC much faster than permanently stored memory in disk files. The more RAM you have the better - up to a point.

Recto The facing side of a page, e.g. page 1 will be recto, page 2 on the reverse is *verso*.

Rivers of Text The effect you get if there is too large a gap between some words. They have a tendency to line up within a paragraph to resemble rivers - can be partially avoided by using only a single space between one sentence and next.

Royalties Payments made by the publisher to the author for the write to publish his or her works. Usually it is a percentage (7-15%) of the sales receipts (not the cover price!)

Scanner A device attached to a PC used to capture a paper-based image such as a photograph. The digital image can then be incorporated into a document.

Self-Publisher Someone who organises, manages, co-ordinates the production, distribution and sales of their own works.

Serial Port Communications port on the back of the PC base unit used for 'serial' devices such as a modem.

Search Engine A database of Internet web pages, News Groups, etc. with a keyword search facility. These are held on very powerful computers and will usually reply to even the most complex search in only a few seconds *(see Alta Vista WWW page)*.

Serif Font A type of font with tails on the characters, e.g. Times. Sans-serif fonts do not have these, e.g. Arial.

Shrink Wrap Plastic film packaging that protects the product - especially on book shop shelves! Requires heat source after initial wrapping and sealing to shrink the plastic tight.

Software Computer programs and packages, e.g. a DTP.

Spreadsheet PC application used for tabulating data in a user friendly way.

Spine The only part of a book seen on a book shelf so try and make it distinctive!

Story-board Roughed out structure of a book to at least sub-heading level.

Style The finishing touches that make your book distinctive and attractive to read: the fonts (typefaces) used, Indentations, spacing, etc.

TLA Three Letter Acronym: No self respecting IT buff would be without them!

TOC Table of Contents: A list of contents with page numbers. Your DTP will be able to generate this for you from the headings and sub-headings used.

Toner The black powder that is consumed by laser printers and photocopiers during the printing process. In laser printers it is normally replaced with a special unit called a toner drum.

Typeface *See font.*

Verso See recto.

Web Browser Software program used to access and view the WWW, e.g. Netscape Navigator and Microsoft Explorer.

Web Page A page or pages of text and images published on the Internet viewable world-wide. This can be you international shop-front and point of contact with customers - design it well!

Web Site A location where a group of web pages are located - typically a disk directory rented from an Internet Provider.

Windows Microsoft operating system. Notable version are 3.x and Windows 95.

WP Word Processing Text-only based forerunner of DTP.

WWW World Wide Web. Page-format information held on the Internet. Accessible via PCs with an account with an Internet Provider. Pages are linked by cross-referencing their URLs.

Unit Cost The cost of producing one book. It includes your materials, labour, overheads and equipment depreciation.

URL Universal Resource Locator. The address of a web page, e.g. http://www.my_name.co.uk/home/

USP Unique Selling Proposition - What makes your product stand out from the crowd!

Vanity Press Such is the desire to see your work in print, you are prepared pay a printer or publisher to produce your book.

10. Appendix

Facts Pages

This book was prepared using the following resources:

PC Hardware

The PC:	• Book started in 1996 using a 1992 model Viglen Vig IV with an Intel 486DX 33Mhz cpu, 8Mb RAM, 340Mb Hard Drive. Running under Window 3.1	*cost in 1992 £4500 + VAT*
	• In Winter of 96/97 the document was transferred to a locally assembled (unbadged) PC with a Cyrix 686 133MHz 150+ CPU with 32Mb of RAM. 1.2Gb Hard disk. 14" monitor. Running under Windows 95.	£1000 inc. VAT
Scanner	Geniscan B&W hand-held with Iphoto & Ipdeluxe software included bought for £129 in 1992, (the equivalent in 1997 would be approximately £60)	£129 inc VAT in 1992. Would be approx. £60in 1997
Printer	• Preparation and draft copies: Canon BCJ 4000 Bubblejet (bought in 1995 for £260 + VAT) capable printing at 360x720dpi in high quality mode.	£260 + VAT in 1995
	• First Production copies: NEC 860 SuperScript laser. 600x1200dpi. 8ppm. Using the booklet printing facilities. (N.B. Toner cartridges £90 approx. covers estimated 5000 pages with 5% ink coverage).	£310 + VAT in 1997

Ancillary Equipment:

Binding	Rexel punch & wirebinding machine	£169 + VAT (1997)
Guillotine	Avery 15" (cuts up to 3mm of paper)	£98 + VAT (1997)

Software

DTP	Commenced with Microsoft Word 6.0 for Windows. Upgraded to version 7.0	free with PC
Clipart	Some images from MS Word package itself, other images from IMSI "101,000 Premium Image Collection".	£39.95 + VAT (1997)
Barcode	Softkey's "Labels Unlimited"	£25.52 + VAT (1997)
Web Page Design	Microsoft Publisher '97 (also used for several illustrations & brochures	£85 + VAT (1997)

Recurrent Production Costs:

Cost per copy (laser printing)	Materials costs (paper, covers, wire binding, laser toner, electricity, equipment depreciation etc.) calculated at per copy. (*This could be substantially reduced by using a more toner- economical printer).	£2.49*

'Liveware'

Authors: experienced with word processor/DTP but not to expert level.
Time taken to write/format/finalise: Approx. 1000 hours over 18 months.

Outside Services

Printer Bureau: CentrePrint , West Street, Leominster, Herefordshire.
Photocopying: currently 6p per double side of A4. *Cover production:* First 2000 covers, £1,150 approx. (Includes printing, laminating, trimming and folding).

Internet Service Providers: U-Net, Warrington, Easy-One plan £12 +VAT per month.

Useful Publications and Further Reading

Ability. Quarterly magazine, covers developments in IT for improving the quality of life for disabled people. Published by The British Computer Society's Disability Group. Contact Room C126, GEC Computer Services Ltd., West Hanningfield Road, Great Baddow, Chelmsford CM2 8HN (Tel. 01245 242950).

Blackwell Guide for Authors . (Blackwell, 1991 revised edition)

BRAD monthly directory (BRAD Maclean Hunter House, Chalk Lane, Cockfosters Road, Barnet EN4 0BU) Lists all newspapers, TV & Commercial Radio Stations, Business Journal - costs over £400 p.a. so visit your local library!.

British Books in Print The Reference Catalogue for Current Literature (published by Whitaker's)

Directory of British Associations (CBD Research Ltd., Chancery House, 15 Wickham Road, Beckenham, Kent, BR3 5JS) - Costs £120, available in libraries

Editing, Design and Book Publishing (Charles Foster, Journeyman Press, 1993). Useful guide written by publishing industry insider.

Guide to Self Publishing (Harry Mullholland , Mulholland/Wirral, 1984)

The Complete Guide to Self-Publishing (Tom & Marilyn Ross, 3 rd edition, Writer's Digest Books, 1994, £12.99 in UK). Comprehensive book (406 pages) covers mainly the North American publishing scene. Good source of contacts for the USA and Canada.

The National Small Press Centre Handbook (How to Publish Books Yourself) (The NSPC Committee, BM BOZO, London WC1N 3XX, 1997) £12. Absolutely Invaluable source book for self-publishers!

How to Publish a Book (Robert Spicer, How To Books, 1995) Useful for source of standard letters to suppliers, distributers, etc.

How to Start a Business from Home , 1995 (Graham Jones, How To Books, 2 nd edition)

A Concise Dictionary of Correct English , 1982 (B.A.Phythian, Hodder and Stoughton)

Copyright And Law for Authors: How to Protect Yourself and Your Creative Work (Helen Shay, How To Books, 1995)

Internet Unleashed (various editors, Sams Net, 1996) Giant of a book covering all aspects of the Internet invaluable source of information for the technically minded.

Marketing for Small Publishers (Bill Godber, Robert Webb, & Keith Smith, Journeyman Press, 1992 2 nd edition). A very useful guide to book marketing.

Marketing Pocket Book annual (NTC Publications, Farm Road, Henley-on-Thames Oxon RG91EJ) Demographic and other marketing statistical data.

The Print Production Handbook (David Bann, Macdonald, 1986) Comprehensive coverage of many aspects of print production .

The Greatest Sales and Marketing Book: The Practical Action Guide for a Small Business. (Peter Hingston 3rd edition, Hingston Associates £7.50) Useful, easy to read guide explaining concepts and principles of marketing.

The Writers Handbook annual (Ed. Barry Turner Macmillan/PEN.) Large handbook containing many hundreds of pages of useful information for the professional and part-time author alike. Advice, anecdotes, names and addresses of agents, publishers, major UK libraries, magazines, newspapers, societies, prizes etc. This book is truly indispensable.

Word for Windows 95 Bible (Heslop and Angell ISBN 1-56884-496-4) IDG Books £38.99. Large authoritative book on Microsoft Word.

The Complete Idiot's Guide to Word for Windows ® *95* (Daniel T Bobola ISBN 0-7897-0378-5) QUE, £18.99. Very good introduction through to intermediate and advanced skill levels.

Teach Yourself PageMaker 6 for Windows 95 (David Browne, ISBN 1-55828-419-2) MIS Press, £22.99. Very good and authoritative guide to this package.

PageMaker in Easy Steps (Scott Basham, ISBN 1-874029-35-0) Computer Step, £7.50. Excellent low price guide, very useful if you have some knowledge of other packages and moving to PageMaker.

Authors and Publishers Associations

American Booksellers Association 828 South Broadway, New York 10591, USA. Tel (914) 591 2665

Association of Learned and Professional Society Publishers, Professor Bernard Donovan, 48 Kelsey Lane, Beckenham, Kent BR3 3NE,. Tel. 0181 658 0459

Association of Little Presses 111 Banbury Road, Oxford, OX2 6XJ see also www.melloworld.com/ alp Support group for small publishers. Membership £12pa.

Independent Publishers Guild 25 Cambridge Road, Hampton, Middlesex TW12 2JL (Tel 0181 979 0250)

Author-Publisher Enterprise, C/O Society of Authors 84 Drayton Gardens, London SW10 9SB Forum and information network for self-publishers.

Booksellers Association of Great Britain and Ireland 272 Vauxhall Bridge Road, London SW1V 1BA (Tel 0171 834 8812) Promotes interests of booksellers, publishes lists and catalogues of members.

The Copyright Licensing Agency Ltd. 90 Tottenham Court Road, London W1P 9HE (Tel 0171 436 3986) Administers, collects and distributes proceeds of copyright fees from photocopying and other reproductions of authors works.

Society of Indexers c/o 38 Rochester Road, London NW1 9JJ, Tel. 0171 916 7809 If you require help creating an index then contact them for advice and contacts.

British Amateur Press Association (BAPA) 78 Tennyson Road, Stratford, London E15 4DR (Tel 0171 555 2052) Promotes amateur mainly 'hobby' press. Provides lots of contacts, resources, etc.

The National Small Press Centre (NSPC) BM Bozo, London WC1N 3XX Promotes interests of small publishers, produces 'News From The Centre' bi-monthly. UK's foremost promoter of small and independent publishers.

Society of Freelance Editors and Proof Readers The Secretary, Mermaid House, 1 Mermaid Court, London (Tel 0171 403 5141) Promotes high standards for its members. Contact for editing and proof-reading see http://www.stepf.demon.co.uk

Society of Young Publishers c/o 12, Dyott Street, London WC1A 1DF Publishes a monthly newsletter called *Inprint* and holds meetings each month.

Writers' Bulletin PO Box 96, Altrincham, Cheshire. WA14 2LN. Resource Bulletin for writers, photographers, cartoonists, etc. invaluable for writers & publishers. Publishes 10 copies per year for £20 subscription.

Suppliers and Services

For your back cover barcodes:
Barcodes Ltd. Vale Road, Portslade, East Sussex BN41 1GD (Tel 01273 422693) (£20 approx + VAT for a barcode, on film or as floppy disk file)

Viking Direct Competitively priced suppliers of stationery, office equipment etc. Next day delivery. Orders can be telephone.

MOPS (Mail Order Protection Schemes) 16 Tooks Court London, EC4A 1LB (Tel 0171 405 6806) Information concerning rules for 'off-the-page' selling in mail order adverts.

Paradigm Technology Ltd. 7 Thames Park, Lester Way, Wallingford, Oxon, OX10 9TA (Tel +44 (0) 1491 822600), email: sales@paratech.co.uk Suppliers of barcode equipment and software, including 'Labels Unlimited'.

Dictation and Voice Activated Software, e.g. Voice Type by IBM available from most software suppliers for about £70 + VAT.

Major Book Suppliers to British Libraries and other library related organisations

BH Blackwell Ltd. Hythe Bridge Street, Oxford, OX1 2ET (Tel 01865 792792)

James Askew & Sons Ltd. 218-222 North Road, Preston PR1 1SY (Tel 01772 555947)

Browns Books, PT Little & Sons Ltd. 22-28 George Street, Kingston-upon-Hull HU1 3AP (Tel 01482 25413)

Bumpus, Haldane & Maxwell Ltd. Olney, Buckinghamshire, MK46 4BN (Tel 01234 711529)

Holt Jackson Book Company Ltd. Preston Road, Lytham, Lancashire FY8 5AX (Tel 01253 737464)

Library Services UK Ltd (formally JMLS Ltd)24 Gamble Street, Nottingham NG7 4FJ (Tel 0115 9708021)

Morley Book Co Elmfield Road, Morley, Leeds LS27 0NN (Tel 01532 538811)

Library Association 7 Ridgemount Street, London WC1E 7AB (Tel 0171 636 7543) For a charge, will supply mailing lists of UK Libraries.

American Library Association (ALA) 50 E. Huron Street, Chicago, IL 60611 (Tel 800 637 0037) . Official association for all US Library, has over 45,000 members.

Public Lending Right Office Bayheath House, Prince Regeant Street, Stockton-on-Tees, Cleveland TS18 1DF (Tel 01642 604699)

Publishing Related Addresses

Book House Training Centre 45 East Hill Wandsworth, London SW18 2QZ (Tel 0181 874 2718/4608)Training centre recognised for promoting excellence in the publishing field. Also acts as a specialised bookseller: Book Publishing Books, invaluable as a source of books on the publishing and book trade.

ISSN Agency, ISSN UK Centre The British Library, Boston Spa, Wetherby, West Yorkshire LS23 7BY (Tel 01937 546958/9) for magazines and serials.

Legal Deposit Office, The British Library Boston Spa, Wetherby, West Yorkshire LS23 7BY (Tel 01937 546612).

Library of Congress Cataloging in Publication Division, Washington, DC 20540.

ISBN Providers

UK: *Bibliographic Services* J Whitaker & Sons Ltd. 12 Dyott Street London WC1A 1DF (Tel. 0171 420 6000 Fax 0171 836 4342 e-mail isbn@whitaker.co.uk.). Will allocate you free ISBNs and disseminate your existence as a publisher to book buyers. Publishes 'The Bookseller' - lists of new publications for the book trade.

Australia: *Australian Standard Book Numbering Agency* , National Library of Australia, Parkes Pl. Canberra ACT 2600.

France: *Éditions du Cercle de la Libraire, Agence Francophone pour la Numérotation Internationale du Livre (AFNIL),* 35 rue Dauphine, 75006 Paris

Netherlands: *Bureau ISBN*, Centraal Bockhuis, Erasmusweg 10, Postbus 360, 4100 AJ Culemborg

USA: *RR Bowker Co.* 121 Chanlon Road, New Providence, NJ 07974 (Tel. 800 526 4902, ext. 2872). ISBN numbers and other publishing resources in the USA. (NB the cost of obtaining ISBNs in the US is currently $115).

Useful Web Pages on the Internet

These sites may be accessed with the http://www prefix.

dibookco.u-net.com Domanski-Irvine Books home page.

altavista.digital.com Alta Vista: very popular search engine for both simple and complex keyword searches.

lycos.com Lycos An alternative and powerful search engine.

hw.ac.uk/scot/research.htm#Computing Sciences source page.

digits.com/web_counter/usage.html Web-counter home page. Lets you create a counter on a web page. Each time someone visits your web site, the counter site increments the count so you can monitor the number of visits you are receiving.

linkcheck.co.uk/writelink/ht/3v_self.htm UK self-publishing link; contains useful self-publishing information.

postbox.com Register here and have your web-site promoted extensively in the USA (but note you will be required to pay for this service.

magazinebusiness.co.uk UK site that lists links to accessible on-line magazines :

yahoo.com/ Yahoo resource, one of the first and best web-site information databases. You can register your web site here.

home.microsoft.com Microsoft's home page, need we say more?

ffg.com/wp/clickbook.html Forefront produces the ClickBooks package that enables booklet and 'n-up' printing regardless of the DTP package and printer. Software can be bought on-line and downloaded from Forefront's web-site.

bookshop.co.uk This is the home page of the On-line Bookshop. Use it to locate and order virtually any book in print by ISBN, Title, author or subject. Your own book(s) will be added to their database via Whitakers book listings. You may add comments about your own books which will be seen on-line by visitors to the site. They also provide a service for book promotion and will add links to your own web site. *This is an invaluable and fast growing resource .*

amazon.com Even bigger on-line bookshop, based in the USA. Provides lots of services and search facilities to the book seeker.

tlt.com/home.html The Literary Times (US) home page. Excellent resource pages. Provides information to help book promotion, e.g. lists of names and addresses of all the major US newspapers.

free.submit-it.com Web site that allows you to insert your www pages into a number of search database for free

unl.ac.uk/SICS/resources.htm School of information resources page. Lists numerous UK and world library resources.

thebookplace.co.uk Book sourcing site owned by Book Data Ltd. Due to go live 1 [st] September 1997. Promises to contain major book title database.

INDEX

Publishing Update December 1998

This update is designed to bring readers up to date with technology, prices and other publishing information. It has been some 18 months since our PC Publishing book was released and, as we predicted, advances computer technology and the fall in costs have continued unabated. Below we provide a summary of prices changes and new developments. Note that prices quoted are exclusive of Value Added Tax (currently 17.5% in the UK).

PC Systems

To sum up, PCs have got faster and cheaper. Now for around £750 + VAT, the discerning buyer can find machines with most of the following specification:

- 233 to 300Mhz Pentium or equivalent processor (ideal for DTP)
- 32 - 64Mb of RAM (The more the better when working with large documents and images)
- 2 - 6 Gb of hard disk space (permanent storage for your files)
- 15 - 17 inch (across the diagonal) monitor (15" now rapidly becoming the standard)
- CD Rom, sound card & speakers as standard

.... And perhaps a 56Kb/sec modem, some suppliers may also throw in an inkjet printer and range of software.

These specifications are at the top of the range or even above those listed in our book and so ideal for DTP and other publishing applications. Prices, overall have fallen by perhaps as much as 40% since last July. The best deals are to be had direct with the supplier / manufacturer rather than the major high street stores. Also note that many towns now have small independent suppliers satisfying local demand and usually quote very keen prices for machines they have assembled themselves.

For those wishing to upgrade their current machine rather than buying a new one, the cost of components has also been falling steadily. The cost of RAM is now less than half the price it was a year ago. Replacement/additional disk drives have similarly fallen in price, a 3Gb drive can be bought for as little as £130, 6Gb for perhaps another £50-60.

Imaging

Scanners

A4 flatbed scanners have dropped in price and the cheapest can now be purchased for well under £100. Note that large images, especially at high resolution are memory, disk and processor hungry. If you intend using lots of images, go for a high spec. PC.

Digital Cameras

Technology continues to evolve quickly for these devices: Take a picture with your camera and download it into your PC for incorporation into documents / web pages. The image quality is improving all the time and the prices are coming down BUT the image quality is not yet as good as conventional photographs.

Printers

Inkjet Printers

Prices have fallen and there is a huge range to choose. Many printers claim to have 'photo-realism' software to produce high quality colour images which some low volume self-publishers may now find are perfectly acceptable for inclusion in their particular publications. Some machines will double up as scanners / fax. You need to be sure what you want. Prices: typical prices are £110 - £500.

Multi-function devices

Several manufacturers have introduced 'multi-function' machines which are aimed at the small office environment. A typical configuration is fax / scanner / printer copier. Usually based around inkjet technology these will scan and print in colour or monochrome, send and receive faxes. Price are around the £250-£500 mark.

Laser Printers

Prices down, quality and speed of printing up. For low volume production (100s - 1000s of booklets, for example), there are now a number of machines capable of printing 16 - 20 pages per minute for less than £1000. As always, look at the cost of consumables - toner cartridges in particular. The cost of printing an A4 page varies between 0.4 and 1.5 pence. Look also at the upgradability of printers, including additional paper bins and duplex attachments (for automatic double-sided printing). At the lower end of the market, perfectly respectable 600 x 600dpm printers capable of printing 8ppm can be had for well under £300.

Alternative Printing Methods

For small numbers of books, the unit cost of printing is high so any developments in technology that provide quality and cost improvements are to be welcomed. One new method of printing now which is of particular interest to the small publisher is 'digital printing' as it is comparatively cheap and has significant advantages over the photocopier. A page is scanned and digitised by a scanner, stored on disk and then multiple copies are made by an ink on paper process - rather than toner transfer via a photoconductive drum. Scanning resolution and printing is high and gives a better copy than photocopying. Cost of prints: will come down as more of these devices are installed but currently about 2/3rds that of photocopying. These printers, however, which can may be able to process both colour and monochrome printing, are seriously expensive. They are beginning to appear widely in print design shops and printing companies so ask around and see what services could be provided locally.

Modems

In our book we suggest that that 14,400kps modems were just about acceptable for web browsing. The standard has moved on. Most modems 'bundled' with PC systems are of the 56kps variety.

Software

Unlike hardware, prices of the top notch packages have only fallen a few percent. Most improvement appears to be in the area of web page authoring. Its getting easier and easier to create high quality pages - important if you intend to publicise your wares on the Internet.

How this book is produced

Production of this book was initially based upon the photocopy method but, although we have never received any complaints, quality assurance was always a bit of a problem. Print quality varied between and within batches and page alignment sometimes less than perfect. Cost of photocopying, as shown in our production costs breakdown, was also the most expensive. Sales of books, however, have now enabled us to upgrade equipment - and practising what we preach, we have bought a rather super HP4000 printer (£711 + VAT) which copes with a variety of paper sizes and thickness and will print double-sided beautifully. It does have a duplexer option (print both sides automatically) but it does slow down the printing process and tends to put more curl in the finished pages. We have found reversing the pages after printing on one side perfectly adequate - and it prints at the full speed of 17ppm. The printer does not come with booklet printing software so we use the ClickBook software package as described in the book. The toner cartridge will print 10,000 sides of A4 paper (at 5% coverage) and so we get over 100 books per cartridge. Printing a book now costs approx. £0.90 in toner and £0.40 in paper. This is less than half the cost of photocopying (but NB. the need to depreciate the cost of equipment and add extra labour, electricity, etc.). The biggest benefit , however, is the excellent and consistent quality of printing.

NOTES